Collins

HANDY
SCOTLAND
ROAD ATLAS

D1012121

Contents

Road maps 2-23
Urban area maps. 24-25
    Aberdeen, Dundee,
    Edinburgh, Glasgow
Index to place names 26-30
Key to street maps 31
    Aberdeen 32-37
    Dundee 38-41
    Edinburgh. 42-57
    Glasgow 58-72
Administrative areas 73

Published by Collins
An imprint of HarperCollins Publishers
77-85 Fulham Palace Road, Hammersmith, London W6 8JB
www.collins.co.uk

Copyright © HarperCollins Publishers Ltd 2006
Collins® is a registered trademark of HarperCollins Publishers Limited
Mapping generated from Collins Bartholomew digital databases

Mapping on pages 32-35, 42-51 and 58-65 uses map data licensed from Ordnance Survey ®
with the permission of the Controller of Her Majesty's Stationery Office.
© Crown copyright. Licence number 399302
The grid on the mapping on pages 24-25, 32-35, 38-39, 42-51 and 58-65 is the National Grid
taken from the Ordnance Survey map with the permission of the Controller of Her Majesty's
Stationery Office.

All rights reserved. No part of this publication may be reproduced, stored in a retrieval
system, or transmitted, in any form or by any means, electronic, mechanical, photocopying,
recording or otherwise, without the prior written permission of the publisher and copyright
owners. The contents of this publication are believed correct at the time of printing.
Nevertheless, the publisher can accept no responsibility for errors or omissions,
changes in the detail given, or for any expense or loss thereby caused.

Key to road map pages

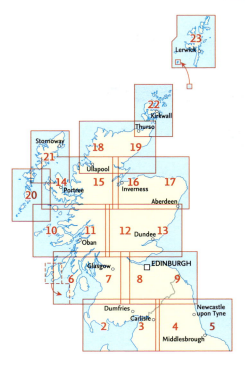

The representation of a road, track or footpath is no evidence of a right of way.

Printed in Hong Kong

ISBN-13   978 0 00720628 5
ISBN-10   0 00 720628 3   Imp 001   TC12158 MDE

e-mail: roadcheck@harpercollins.co.uk

A

14

B

Rum (Rhum)
Kinloch

Aird of Sleat
Point of Sleat

C

Sound of

Askival
812

Sound of Rum

Rubha nam Meirleach

Cleadale

Eigg
An Sgurr
393
Galmisdale

Eilean nan Each

Sound of Eigg

Ari

Sound of A

Muck

Eilean Shona

Lochboisdale

Ockle

Ardtoe

Acha

I N N E R

Castlebay

Point of Ardnamurchan

Achosnich

Ardnamurchan

Eilean Mor

B8007

Ben Hiant
528

Sorisdale

Kilchoan

Glenbeg

H E B R I D E S

B8072

Clabhach

Coll

Ardmore Point

Glenborrodale

B8071

Arinagour

Caliach Point

Tobermory

Drimnin

M

12

B8070

Loch Eatharna

Calgary

B8017

Dervaig

Loch Frisa

Killundine

Arie

Gunna

Crossapol Bay

Calgary Bay

B8849

Fiur

Hough Bay

B8068
B8069
Caolas

Tiree

Kilninian

Loch Tuath

Salen

A848

23

A849

Barrapoll

B8065

Tiree
Scarinish

Treshnish Isles

Gometra

Lagganulva
Ulva

B8073

B8035

Knock

Loch Ba

L
G

Balephuil

Balemartine

Hynish Bay

Little Colonsay

Staffa

Balnahard

Mull

Ben More
966

B8035

Glen More

IONA ABBEY

Sound of Iona

Baile Mòr
Iona

Fionnphort

A849

Loch Scridain

35

Ben Buie
717

Pennyghael

Bunessan

Carsaig

Loch Buie

Soa Island

Ross of Mull

Ardchiavaig

Malcolm's Point

Fi

Garve

Sca

Kiloran Bay

Rubh' a' Geodha

Colonsay

B8086
Kiloran

Kilchattan

Scalasaig

Loch Staosnaig

A

6

B

Jarvard

B8085

(summ

C

ainn Bhreac
467

Dubh Eilean

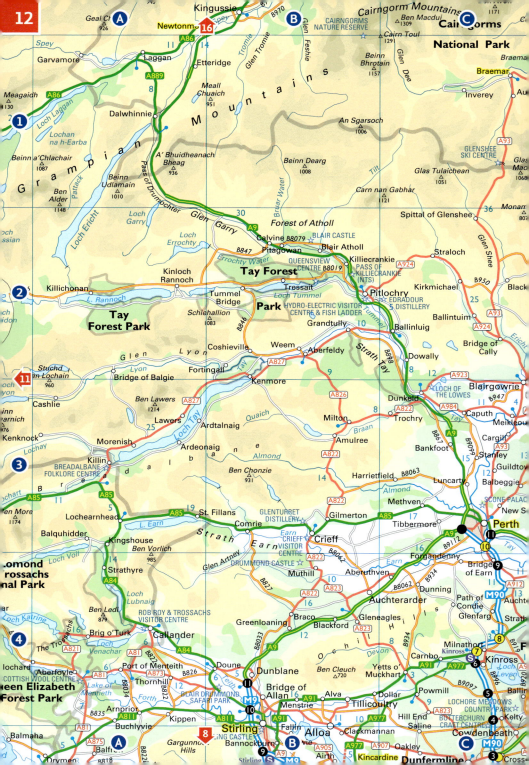

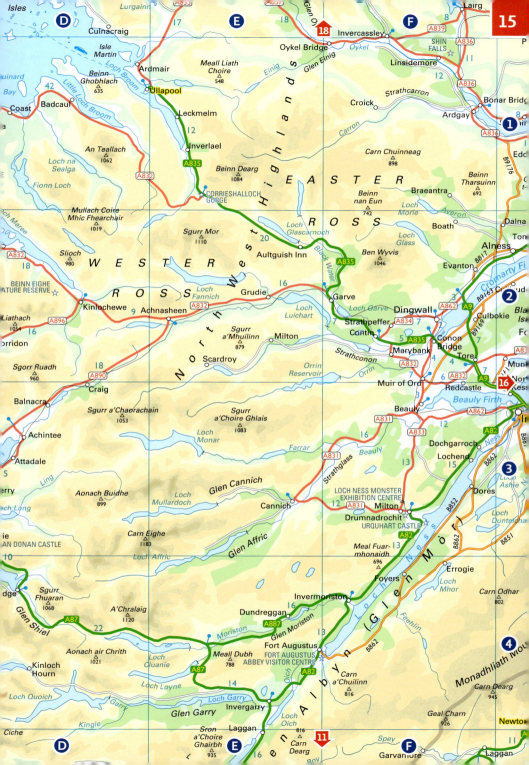

SHETLAND ISLANDS

D E F

1

Herma Ness
Burrafirth
Valsgarth
Haroldswick
Unst
Baltasound
10

Cullivoe
Belmont
Gutcher
Uyeasound
Sellafirth
A968

Yell

A968
18
Oddsta
Fetlar
B9088 Houbie

Point of Fethaland

North Roe
Mid Yell
Hascosay
The Faither
West Sandwick
Funzie
A970
Ronas Hill 450
Collafirth
Otterswick
Aywick
Ollaberry
West Yell
A968
Urafirth
Esha Ness
B9078
Ulsta
Hamnavoe
Stenness
Hillswick
A970
17
Burravoe
Toft
St. Magnus Bay
Mossbank

2

Out Skerries

B9076
10
A968
Brae
Lunna
Skaw
Whalsay
Muckle Roe
Hillside
Brough
Vidlin
Isbister
Voe
Laxo
B9071
B9071
Dury Voe
Symbister
A970
Papa Stour
B9075
South Nesting Bay

3

Sandness
A971
Aith
B9075
20
Bridge of Walls
Bixter
Setter
Weisdale
B9071
Girlsta
Walls
Garderhouse
Whiteness
Culswick
Skeld
Veensgarth
Lerwick
Isle of Ness
Scalloway
Bressay
Hamnavoe
B9074
Quarff
Bergen, Seydisfjordur & Torshavn (summer only)

4

Burra (West Burra)
Cunningsburgh
Fair Isle
Sandwick
Mousa
Stonybreck
Hoswick
Bigton
B9122
Levenwick
A970
Scousburgh
Boddam
Toab
Sumburgh
Grutness
JARLSHOF
Sumburgh
Sumburgh Head
Kirkwall & Aberdeen

D E F

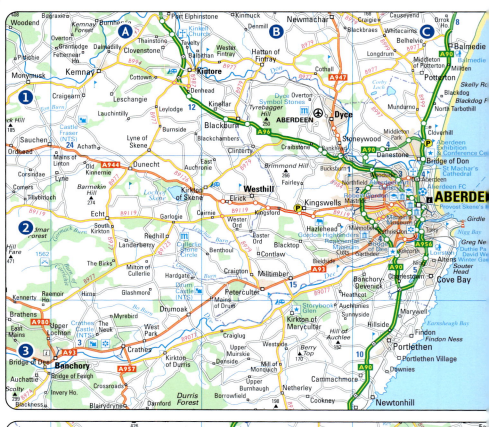

Administrative area abbreviations

Aber.	Aberdeenshire	*E.Dun.*	East Dunbartonshire	*Ork.*	Orkney	*Stir.*	Stirling
Arg. & B.	Argyll & Bute	*Edin.*	Edinburgh	*P. & K.*	Perthshire & Kinross	*T. & W.*	Tyne & Wear
Cumb.	Cumbria	*High.*	Highland	*S.Ayr.*	South Ayrshire	*W.Dun.*	West Dunbartonshire
D. & G.	Dumfries & Galloway	*Midloth.*	Midlothian	*S.Lan.*	South Lanarkshire	*W. Isles*	Western Isles
Dur.	Durham	*N.Lan.*	North Lanarkshire	*Sc.Bord.*	Scottish Borders		(Na h-Eileanan an Iar)
E.Ayr.	East Ayrshire	*Northumb.*	Northumberland	*Shet.*	Shetland	*W. Loth.*	West Lothian

Index entries shown in **bold** type can be found on the urban area maps, pages 24–25

A
Abbeytown 3 E2
Aberchirder 17 D2
Aberdeen 17 F4
Aberdeen 24 C2
Aberdeen Airport 17 E4
Aberdeen Airport 24 B1
Aberdour 8 B1
Aberfeldy 12 B2
Aberfoyle 12 A4
Aberlady 8 C1
Aberlemno 13 E2
Aberlour 16 C3
Abernethy 12 C4
Aberuthven 12 C4
Abhainnsuidhe 21 D3
Abington 8 A3
Aboyne 17 D4
Abronhill 25 F1
Achadh Mòr 21 E2
Achahoish 6 C1
Acharacle 10 C2
Achath 24 A1
Achavanich 19 E2
Achfary 18 B2
Achiltibuie 18 A3
Achintee 15 D3
Achnacroish 11 D3
Achnasheen 15 E2
Achosnich 10 C2
Achriesgill 18 B2
Acomb 4 B1
Aird Asaig 21 D3
Aird of Sleat 14 B4
Airdrie 7 G2
Airdrie 25 F2
Airidh a'Bhruaich 21 E2
Airth 8 A1
Aith *Ork.* 22 C2
Aith *Shet.* 23 E3
Akeld 9 E3
Alexandria 7 E1
Alford 17 D4
Allanton *N.Lan.* 8 A2
Allanton *S.Lan.* 25 F3
Allendale Town 4 B2
Allenheads 4 B2
Allnabad 18 C2
Alloa 12 B4
Allonby 3 E2
Alloway 7 E3
Alness 16 A2
Alnmouth 9 F4
Alnwick 9 F4
Alston 4 A2
Altens 24 C2
Altnafeadh 11 F2
Altnaharra 18 C2
Alva 12 B4
Alves 16 B2
Alvie 16 A4
Alyth 13 D2
Amble 9 F4
Ambleside 3 F4
Amulree 12 B3
An Tairbeart (Tarbert) 21 E3
Ancroft 9 E2
Ancrum 9 D3
Andreas 2 B4
Annan 3 E1
Annbank 7 E3
Annfield Plain 4 C2
Anniesland 25 D2
Anstruther 13 E4
Aoradh 6 A3
Appleby-in-Westmorland 4 A3
Applecross 14 C3
Arbirlot 13 E3
Arbroath 13 E3
Ardchiavaig 10 B4
Arden 7 E1

Ardentinny 7 E1
Ardeonaig 12 A3
Ardersier 16 A2
Ardfern 11 D4
Ardgay 18 C4
Ardlui 11 F4
Ardlussa 6 B1
Ardmair 18 A4
Ardminish 6 B2
Ardmolich 11 D1
Ardrishaig 6 C1
Ardrossan 7 E2
Ardtalnaig 12 A3
Ardtoe 10 C2
Ardvasar 14 C4
Arinagour 10 B2
Arisaig 10 C1
Armadale 8 A1
Arnisdale 14 C4
Arniston Engine 25 F5
Arnol 21 E1
Arnprior 12 A4
Arrochar 11 F4
Ashgill 25 F3
Ashington 5 D1
Ashkirk 8 C3
Aspatria 3 E2
Attadale 15 D3
Auchallater 12 C1
Auchenback 25 D3
Auchenblae 13 E1
Auchenbreck 6 D1
Auchencairn 3 D2
Auchencrow 9 E2
Auchendinny 25 E5
Auchindrain 11 E4
Auchinleck 7 F3
Auchinloch 25 E1
Auchlunies 24 B3
Auchmull 13 E1
Auchnagatt 17 F3
Aucholzie 13 D1
Auchterarder 12 B4
Auchterhouse 24 A4
Auchtermuchty 13 D4
Auchtertool 8 B1
Auldearn 16 B2
Auldhouse 25 E3
Aultbea 15 D1
Aultguish Inn 15 E2
Aviemore 16 B4
Avoch 16 A2
Avonbridge 8 A1
Aycliffe 5 D3
Ayr 7 E3
Aysgarth 4 C4
Aywick 23 F2

B
Backaland 22 B2
Badcaul 18 A4
Badenscoth 17 E3
Badintagairt 18 B3
Badlipster 19 F2
Bàgh a'Chaisteil (Castlebay) 20 A4
Baile Mhartainn 20 A1
Baile Mòr 10 B3
Baillieston 25 E2
Bainbridge 4 B4
Balallan 21 E2
Balbeggie 12 C3
Balbithan 24 A1
Balblair 16 A2
Baldernock 25 D1
Baldovan 24 A4
Baldovie 24 B4
Balemartine 10 A3
Balephuil 10 A3
Balerno 25 D5
Balfour 22 B3
Balfron 7 F1
Balgown 14 B2
Balhelvie 24 A5

Balintore 16 A2
Balivanich 20 A2
Ballachulish 11 E2
Ballantrae 2 A1
Ballater 13 D1
Ballaugh 2 B4
Ballingry 12 C4
Ballinluig 12 C2
Ballintuim 12 C2
Balloch *N.Lan.* 25 F1
Balloch *W.Dun.* 7 E1
Ballochan 13 D1
Ballochroy 6 C2
Ballygrant 6 A2
Balmacara 14 C3
Balmaha 7 E1
Balmedie 17 F4
Balmedie 24 C1
Balmerino 24 A5
Balmore 25 E1
Balmullo 24 B5
Balnacra 15 D3
Balnahard 10 C3
Balnapaling 16 A2
Balquhidder 12 A3
Baltasound 23 F1
Balvicar 11 D4
Bamburgh 9 F3
Banchory 13 E1
Banchory 24 A3
Banchory-Devenick 24 C2
Banff 17 E2
Bankfoot 12 C3
Bankhead 24 B1
Bannockburn 8 A1
Barassie 7 E3
Barbaraville 16 A2
Bardowie 25 D1
Bargeddie 25 E2
Bargrennan 2 B1
Barnard Castle 4 C3
Barnhill 24 B4
Barnton 25 D4
Barr 7 E4
Barrapoll 10 A3
Barrhead 7 F2
Barrhill 2 B1
Barrock 19 F1
Barry 24 C4
Barvas 21 E1
Bathgate 8 A1
Beadnell 9 F3
Bearsden 7 F2
Bearsden 25 D1
Beattock 8 B4
Beauly 15 F3
Bedale 5 D4
Bedlington 4 C1
Beith 7 E2
Belford 9 F3
Belhelvie 24 C1
Bellingham 4 B1
Bellshill 7 G2
Bellshill 25 F2
Belmont 23 F1
Belsay 4 C1
Benthoul 24 B2
Benvie 24 A4
Bernisdale 14 B2
Berriedale 19 E3
Berwick-upon-Tweed 9 E2
Bettyhill 18 C1
Bieldside 24 B2
Biggar 8 A3
Bigton 23 E4
Bilbster 19 F2
Billingham 5 D3
Billy Row 4 C2
Bilston 8 B2
Bilston 25 E5
Bimbister 22 B3
Birdston 25 E1

Birkhill 24 A4
Birsay 22 A2
Birtley 5 D2
Bishop Auckland 4 C3
Bishopbriggs 7 F1
Bishopbriggs 25 E1
Bishopton 7 F1
Bixter 23 E3
Blackbraes 24 B1
Blackburn *Aber.* 17 E4
Blackburn *Aber.* 24 B1
Blackburn *W.Loth.* 8 A2
Blackchambers 24 A1
Blackdog 24 C1
Blackford 12 B4
Blackhall 25 E4
Blackhall Colliery 5 D2
Blacklunans 12 C2
Blackridge 8 A1
Blacktop 24 B2
Blackwaterfoot 6 C3
Blaich 11 E1
Blair Atholl 12 B2
Blairgowrie 12 C3
Blairydryne 24 A3
Blantyre 25 E3
Blaydon 4 C1
Blyth 5 D1
Blyth Bridge 8 B2
Boat of Garten 16 B4
Boath 15 F2
Boddam *Aber.* 17 F3
Boddam *Shet.* 23 E4
Bogniebrae 17 D3
Bograxie 24 A1
Boldon 5 D2
Boltby 5 D4
Bolton 8 C1
Bonar Bridge 18 C4
Bonawe 11 E3
Bonawe Quarries 11 E3
Bonchester Bridge 9 D4
Bo'ness 8 A1
Bonjedward 9 D3
Bonnington 25 D5
Bonnybridge 8 A1
Bonnyrigg 8 C2
Bonnyrigg 25 F5
Bonnyton (East) *Angus* 24 C4
Bonnyton (West) *Angus* 24 A4
Bootle 3 E4
Boreland 8 B4
Boreraig 14 A2
Borgh 20 A4
Borgue *D. & G.* 2 C2
Borgue *High.* 19 E3
Borrowdale 3 F3
Borrowfield 24 B3
Borve *High.* 14 B3
Borve *W.Isles* 21 E1
Bothel 3 E2
Bothwell 25 F3
Bottomcraig 24 A5
Bournmoor 5 D2
Bow 22 B3
Bowburn 5 D2
Bowes 4 B3
Bowmore 6 A2
Bowness-on-Solway 3 E1
Bowness-on-Windermere 3 F4
Bracadale 14 A3
Braco 12 B4
Bracora 11 D1
Brae 23 E2
Braeantra 15 F1
Braehead 25 D2
Braemar 12 C1
Bragar 21 E1
Braithwaite 3 E3
Brampton 4 A2

Brandon 4 C2
Breakish 14 C4
Breanais 21 D2
Breascleit 21 E2
Brechin 13 E2
Bridge of Allan 12 B4
Bridge of Balgie 12 A2
Bridge of Cally 12 C2
Bridge of Craigisla 13 D2
Bridge of Don 17 F4
Bridge of Don 24 C2
Bridge of Dun 13 E2
Bridge of Dye 13 E1
Bridge of Earn 12 C4
Bridge of Orchy 11 F3
Bridge of Walls 23 E3
Bridge of Weir 7 E2
Bridgefoot 24 A4
Bridgend *Angus* 13 E2
Bridgend (Islay) *Arg. & B.* 6 A2
Bridgend (Lochgilphead) *Arg. & B.* 6 C1
Bridgend *Moray* 16 C3
Bridgeton 25 E2
Brig o'Turk 12 A4
Brigham 3 E3
Brinian 22 B2
Broadford 14 C4
Brochel 14 B3
Brodick 6 D3
Brompton 5 D4
Brompton on Swale 4 C4
Brora 19 D4
Brotton 5 E3
Brough *Cumb.* 4 B3
Brough *High.* 19 E1
Brough *Shet.* 23 F2
Broughton 8 B3
Broughton in Furness 3 E4
Broughtown 22 C2
Broughty Ferry 13 E3
Broughty Ferry 24 B4
Broxburn 8 B1
Brunton 24 A5
Buchlyvie 12 A4
Buckhaven 13 D4
Buckie 17 D2
Bucklerheads 24 B4
Bucksburn 17 E4
Bucksburn 24 B2
Buddon 24 C4
Buldoo 19 E1
Bunessan 10 B3
Burgh by Sands 3 F2
Burghead 16 B2
Burness 22 C2
Burnhervie 24 A1
Burnhouse 7 E2
Burniston 5 F4
Burnmouth 9 E2
Burnopfield 4 C2
Burnside 24 A1
Burnside of Duntrune 24 B4
Burntisland 8 B1
Burrafirth 23 F1
Burravoe 23 F2
Burrelton 12 C3
Burwick 22 B4
Busby 25 D3
Buttermere 3 E3

C
Cadder 25 E1
Cadzow 25 F3
Cairnbaan 6 C1
Cairndow 11 E4
Cairneyhill 8 A1
Cairnie 24 B2
Cairnryan 2 A1
Caldbeck 3 F2
Calderbank 25 F2

aldercruix 8 A1
Alderglen 25 E3
Caldwell 4 C3
alfsound 22 B2
algary 10 B2
allander 12 A4
allanish 21 E2
alvine 12 B2
amasnacroise 11 D2
Cambuslang 25 E2
Cammachmore 24 C3
ampbeltown 6 C3
amps 25 D5
amptown 9 D4
annich 15 E3
anonbie 3 F1
aolas 10 A2
appercleuch 8 B3
applegill 8 B4
aputh 12 C3
arbost (Loch Snizort
    Beag) High. 14 B3
arbost (Loch Harport)
    High. 14 B3
arbrain 25 F1
ardenden 13 D4
Cardonald 25 D2
ardross 7 E1
arfin 25 F3
argenbridge 3 D1
argill 12 C3
arlisle 3 F2
arlops 8 B2
arloway 21 E1
arluke 8 A2
armunnock 25 D3
armyle 25 E2
armyllie 13 E3
arnbee 13 E4
arnbo 12 C4
arnoustie 13 E3
arnoustie 24 C4
arntyne 25 E2
arnwath 8 A2
arradale 6 C3
arrbridge 16 B4
arrington 25 F5
arronbridge 8 A4
arsaig 10 C3
arsluith 2 C2
arsphairn 7 F4
arstairs 8 A2
ashlie 12 A3
Castle Carrock 4 A2
astle Douglas 3 D2
astle Kennedy 2 A2
astlebay (Bàgh a'
    Chaisteil) 20 A4
astlemilk 25 E3
astleside 4 C2
astleton 5 E4
astletown 19 E1
athcart 25 D2
athkin 25 E3
atrine 7 F3
atterick 4 C4
atterick Camp 4 C4
Causeyend 24 C1
awdor 16 A2
Ceann a' Bhàigh 20 A1
earsiadar 21 E2
eres 13 D4
hampany 8 A1
Chapelhall 25 F2
harlestown 17 F4
Charlestown 24 C2
hatton 9 E3
hester-le-Street 5 D2
hesters 9 D4
hilton 5 D3
hirnside 9 E2
hopwell 4 C2
hriston Bank 9 F3
hryston 7 G1
Chryston 25 E1
ille Bhrìghde 20 A3
labhach 10 A2
lachan (Loch Fyne)
    Arg. & B. 11 E4
lachan (Kintyre)
    Arg. & B. 6 C2
lachan High. 14 B3
lachan of Glendaruel
    6 D1
lachtolt 18 A3
Clackmannan 8 A1
ladich 11 E3

Claggan 11 D2
Claonaig 6 C2
Clarkston 25 D3
Clashmore 16 A1
Clashnessie 18 A3
Cleadale 10 C1
Cleadon 5 D1
Cleat 22 B4
Cleator Moor 3 E3
Cleland 8 A2
Cleland 25 F3
Clermiston 25 D4
Clestrain 22 A3
Clinterty 24 B1
Closeburn 8 A4
Cloughton 5 F4
Clova 13 D1
Clovenfords 8 C2
Clovenstone 24 A1
Cloverhill 24 C1
Clovullin 11 E2
Clunes 11 F1
Clydebank 7 F1
Coalburn 8 A3
Coast 15 D1
Coatbridge 7 G2
Coatbridge 25 F2
Cock Bridge 16 C4
Cockburnspath 9 D1
Cockenzie & Port Seton
    8 C1
Cockermouth 3 E3
Cockfield 4 C3
Cockpen 25 F5
Coldingham 9 E2
Coldstream 9 E3
Colinton 25 E5
Colintraive 6 D1
Collafirth 23 E2
Collieston 17 F3
Collin 3 E1
Colmonell 2 A1
Colnabaichin 16 C4
Colquhar 8 C2
Comrie 12 B3
Condorrat 25 F1
Coniston 3 F4
Connel 11 D3
Conon Bridge 15 F2
Consett 4 C2
Contin 15 F2
Contlaw 24 B2
Cookney 24 B3
Copley 4 C3
Corbridge 4 B1
Cornhill 17 D2
Cornhill-on-Tweed 9 E3
Corpach 11 E2
Corrie 6 D2
Corsock 3 D1
Corstorphine 25 D4
Coshieville 12 B2
Cothall 24 B1
Cottown 24 A1
Coulport 7 E1
Coultra 24 A5
Coundon 4 C3
Coupar Angus 13 D3
Cousland 25 F5
Cove Arg. & B. 7 E1
Cove High. 14 C1
Cove Bay 7 F3
Cove Bay 24 C2
Cowdenbeath 8 B1
Cowie 8 A1
Cowshill 4 B2
Coylton 7 E3
Coylumbridge 16 B4
Craibstone 24 B1
Craichie 13 D2
Craig 15 D3
Craigandaive 7 D1
Craigdarroch 7 F4
Craigearn 24 A1
Craigellachie 16 C3
Craigendoran 7 E1
Craighat 7 F1
Craigie Aber. 24 C1
Craigie Dundee 24 B4
Craiglockhart 25 E4
Craiglug 24 B3
Craigmillar 25 E4
Craigneuk 25 F3
Craignure 11 D3
Craigton Aberdeen
    24 B2
Craigton Angus 24 C4

Crail 13 E4
Cramlington 5 D1
Cramond 8 B1
Cramond 25 D4
Cranshaws 9 D2
Crask Inn 18 C3
Craster 9 F3
Crathes 24 A3
Crathie 13 D1
Crawfordjohn 8 A3
Creagorry 20 B2
Creetown 2 C2
Creich 24 A5
Crianlarich 11 F3
Crichton 25 F5
Crieff 12 B3
Crimond 17 F2
Crinan 11 D4
Crocketford (Ninemile
    Bar) 3 D1
Croick 15 F1
Cromarty 16 A2
Crombie Mill 24 C4
Crook 4 C3
Crookham 9 E3
Crosbost 21 E2
Crosby Ravensworth
    4 A3
Crossaig 6 C2
Crosscanonby 3 E2
Crossford Fife 8 B1
Crossford S.Lan. 8 A2
Crossgatehall 25 F5
Crossgates 8 B1
Crosshands 7 F3
Crosshill 7 E4
Crosshouse 7 E3
Crossmichael 2 C1
Crossroads 24 A3
Croy High. 16 A3
Croy N.Lan. 7 G1
Croy N.Lan. 25 F1
Cruden Bay 17 F3
Crùlabhig 21 E2
Crutherland Farm 25 E3
Culbokie 15 F2
Culdrain 17 D3
Cullen 17 D2
Cullicudden 16 A2
Cullipool 11 D4
Cullivoe 23 F1
Culnacraig 18 A4
Culnaknock 14 B2
Culross 8 A1
Culswick 23 E3
Cults 17 E4
Cults 24 B2
Cumbernauld 7 G1
Cumbernauld 25 F1
Cuminestown 17 E2
Cumnock 7 F3
Cunningsburgh 23 E4
Cupar 13 D4
Currie 25 D5

D
Dacre 3 F3
Dailly 7 E4
Dairsie 13 D4
Dalabrog 20 A3
Dalbeattie 3 D2
Dalgety Bay 8 B1
Dalkeith 8 C1
Dalkeith 25 F5
Dallas 16 B2
Dalmadilly 24 A1
Dalmally 11 E3
Dalmellington 7 F4
Dalmeny 25 D4
Dalnavie 16 A2
Dalry 7 E2
Dalrymple 7 E4
Dalserf 25 F3
Dalston 3 F2
Dalwhinnie 12 A1
Danby 5 E4
Danderhall 25 F5
Danestone 24 C1
Darlington 5 D3
Darnford 24 A3
Darra 17 E3
Darvel 7 F3
Dava 16 B3
Daviot 16 A3
Dearham 3 E3
Dechmont 8 A1
Denhead 24 A1

Denhead of Gray 24 A4
Denholm 9 D3
Denmill 24 B1
Denny 8 A1
Denside 24 B3
Dervaig 10 C2
Dhoon 2 B4
Dingwall 15 F2
Dinnet 17 D4
Dippen 6 C3
Dirleton 8 C1
Distington 3 E3
Dochgarroch 15 F3
Doddington 9 E3
Dollar 12 B4
Dolphinton 8 B2
Dores 15 F3
Dornie 15 D3
Dornoch 16 A1
Dougalston 25 D1
Dougarie 6 C3
Douglas 8 A3
Douglas & Angus 24 B4
Douglastown 13 D2
Dounby 22 A3
Doune 12 B4
Dounreay 19 E1
Dowally 12 C2
Downfield 24 A4
Downies 24 C3
Dreghorn 7 E3
Drem 8 C1
Drimnin 10 C2
Drongan 7 F3
Dronley 24 A4
Druimdrishaig 6 C1
Drumbeg 18 A3
Drumchapel 25 D1
Drumclog 7 F3
Drumlithie 13 F1
Drummore 2 A2
Drumnadrochit 15 F3
Drumoak 24 A3
Drumsturdy 24 B4
Drymen 7 F1
Duchally 18 B3
Duddingston 25 E4
Duddo 9 E2
Dufftown 16 C3
Duirinish 14 C3
Dullatur 25 F1
Dulnain Bridge 16 B3
Dumbarton 7 E1
Dumfries 3 E1
Dunbar 9 D1
Dunbeath 19 E3
Dunblane 12 B4
Dundee 13 D3
Dundee 24 B4
Dundee Airport 24 A5
Dundonald 7 E3
Dundreggan 15 E4
Dundrennan 3 D2
Dunecht 17 E4
Dunecht 24 A2
Dunfermline 8 B1
Dunkeld 12 C3
Dunlop 7 E2
Dunnet 19 E1
Dunning 12 C4
Dunoon 7 E1
Dunragit 2 A2
Duns 9 D2
Dunscore 3 D1
Dunure 7 E3
Dunvegan 14 A3
Durham 5 D2
Durham Tees Valley
    Airport 5 D3
Durness 18 B1
Dyce 17 E4
Dyce 24 B1
Dyke 16 B2
Dykehead 13 D2

E
Eaglescliffe 5 D3
Eaglesfield 3 E1
Eaglesham 7 F2
Eaglesham 25 D3
Earlston 9 D3
Earsairidh 20 A4
Easdale 11 D4
Easington 5 D2
Easington Colliery 5 D2
East Auchronie 24 B2
East Calder 8 B1

East Haven 13 E3
East Haven 24 C4
East Kilbride 7 F2
East Kilbride 25 E3
East Linton 9 D1
East March 24 B4
East Wemyss 13 E4
Easter Knox 24 C4
Easter Lednathie 13 D2
Easter Ord 24 B2
Easterhouse 25 E2
Eastgate 4 B2
Easthouses 25 F5
Eastriggs 3 F1
Ecclaw 9 D1
Ecclefechan 3 E1
Eccles 9 D2
Echt 17 E4
Echt 24 A2
Eckford 9 D3
Edderton 16 A1
Eddleston 8 B2
Eddlewood 25 F3
Edgehead 25 F5
Edinburgh 8 B1
Edinburgh 25 E4
Edinburgh Airport 8 B1
Edinburgh Airport
    25 D4
Edlingham 9 F4
Edmundbyers 4 C2
Edzell 13 E2
Egglescliffe 5 D3
Eglingham 9 F3
Egremont 3 E3
Egton 5 F4
Einacleit 21 D2
Elgin 16 C2
Elgol 14 B4
Elie 13 E4
Ellingham 9 F3
Ellington 9 F4
Ellon 17 F3
Elphin 18 B3
Elphinstone 25 F4
Elrick 24 B2
Elsdon 9 E4
Elsrickle 8 B2
Elvanfoot 8 A3
Embleton 9 F3
Enterkinfoot 8 A4
Eoropaidh 21 F1
Eriboll 18 B2
Errogie 15 F4
Errol 13 D3
Esh Winning 4 C2
Eskbank 25 F5
Eskdalemuir 8 B4
Eston 5 E3
Etteridge 12 A1
Ettrick 8 B4
Ettrickbridge 8 C3
Evanton 15 F2
Eyemouth 9 E2

F
Faifley 25 D1
Fairhill 25 F3
Fairholm 25 F3
Fairley 24 B2
Fairlie 7 E2
Fairmilehead 25 E5
Falkirk 8 A1
Falkland 13 D4
Fallin 8 A1
Falstone 4 A1
Farr 16 A3
Fauldhouse 8 A2
Fearnmore 14 C2
Felling 5 D1
Felton 9 F4
Fenwick E.Ayr. 7 F2
Fenwick Northumb. 9 F2
Feochaig 6 C4
Feolin Ferry 6 B1
Fern 13 E2
Ferness 16 B3
Ferryden 13 E2
Ferryhill 5 D3
Feshiebridge 16 A4
Fettercairn 13 E1
Fetternear House
    24 A1
Finavon 13 E2
Findhorn 16 B2
Findochty 17 D2

Findon 24 C3
Finnygaud 17 D2
Finstown 22 B3
Fintry 7 F1
Fionnphort 10 B3
Fishburn 5 D3
Fishnish 10 C3
Fiunary 10 C2
Flemington 25 E3
Flimby 3 E3
Flodden 9 E3
Fochabers 16 C2
Ford *Arg. & B.* 11 D4
Ford *Midloth.* **25 F5**
Ford *Northumb.* 9 E3
Fordoun 13 F1
Fordyce 17 D2
Forfar 13 D2
Forgandenny 12 C3
Forgie 16 C2
Forres 16 B2
Forsinard 19 D2
Fort Augustus 15 E4
Fort William 11 E1
Forth 8 A2
Fortingall 12 B2
Fortrose 16 A2
Foulden 9 E2
Fowlis 24 A4
Foyers 15 F4
Fraserburgh 17 F2
Freswick 19 F1
Freuchie 13 D4
Friockheim 13 E2
Frizington 3 E3
Funzie 23 F1
Furnace 11 E4
Fyvie 17 E3

G
Gainford 4 C3
Gairloch 14 C1
Galashiels 8 C1
Galmisdale 10 C1
Galston 7 F3
Gardenstown 17 E2
Garderhouse 23 E3
Garelochhead 7 E1
Garlieston 2 C2
Garlogie 24 A2
Garsdale Head 4 B4
Gartcosh 25 E2
Garthdee 24 C2
Gartocharn 7 F1
Garvald 9 D1
Garvamore 12 A1
Garvard 6 A1
Garve 15 F2
Gatehouse of Fleet 2 C2
Gateshead 5 D2
Gauldry 24 A5
Gawthrop 4 A4
Gearraidh na h-Aibhne
   21 F2
Giffnock 7 F2
Giffnock 25 D3
Gifford 8 C1
Gillamoor 5 E4
Gilling West 4 C4
Gilmerton *Edin.* **25 E5**
Gilmerton *P. & K.* 12 B3
Gilsland 4 A1
Gilston 8 C2
Girlsta 23 E3
Girvan 7 E4
Glamis 13 D2
Glanton 9 E3
Glasgow 7 F2
Glasgow 25 D2
Glasgow Airport 7 F2
Glasgow Prestwick
   International Airport
   7 E3
Glashmore 24 A2
Glassford 7 G2
Glenbarr 6 C3
Glenbeg 10 C2
Glenboig 25 F2
Glenborrodale 10 C2
Glenbreck 8 B3
Glenbrittle 14 B4
Glencaple 3 E1
Glencarse 12 C3
Glencoe 11 E2
Gleneagles 12 B4
Glenegedale 6 A2
Glenelg 14 C4

Glenfarg 12 C4
Glenfinnan 11 D1
Glengarnock 7 E2
Glenkindie 17 D4
Glenluce 2 A2
Glenmavis 25 F2
Glenrothes 13 D4
Gogar 25 D4
Golspie 19 D4
Gordon 9 D2
Gorebridge 8 C2
Gorebridge 25 F5
Gorgie 25 E4
Gosforth *Cumb.* 3 E4
Gosforth *T. & W.* 4 C1
Gourdon 13 F2
Govan 25 D2
Gowkthrapple 25 F3
Grabhair 21 E2
Grandtully 12 B2
Grangemouth 8 A1
Grantlodge 24 A1
Granton 25 E4
Grantown-on-Spey
   16 B3
Grantshouse 9 E2
Grasmere 3 F4
Grayrigg 4 A4
Great Ayton 5 E3
Great Broughton 5 E4
Great Clifton 3 E3
Great Salkeld 4 A2
Greenfaulds 25 F1
Greengairs 7 G1
Greengairs 25 F1
Greenhead 4 A1
Greenigo 22 B3
Greenlaw 9 D2
Greenloaning 12 B4
Greenock 7 E1
Gress 21 F1
Gretna 3 F1
Greystoke 3 F3
Gritley 22 B3
Grizebeck 3 E4
Grudie 15 E2
Grutness 23 E4
Guide Post 4 C1
Guildtown 12 C3
Guisborough 5 E3
Gullane 8 C1
Gutcher 23 F1

H
Hackness 5 F4
Haddington 8 C1
Halkirk 19 E2
Hall 7 E2
Haltwhistle 4 A1
Ham 23 D3
Hamilton 7 G2
Hamilton 25 F3
Hamnavoe (Mainland)
   Shet. 23 E4
Hamnavoe (Yell) *Shet.*
   23 F2
Harbost 21 F1
Hardgate 24 A2
Haroldswick 23 F1
Harrietfield 12 C3
Harthill 8 A2
Hartlepool 5 E3
Hassendean 8 C3
Haswell 5 D2
Hatton 17 F3
**Hatton of Fintray
   24 B1**
Haugh of Urr 3 D1
Hawes 4 B4
Hawick 8 C3
Hawkshead 3 F4
Haydon Bridge 4 B1
Hazelton Walls 24 A5
Hazlehead 24 B2
Healeyfield 4 C2
Heathcot 24 B2
Hebburn 5 D1
Helensburgh 7 E1
Helmsdale 19 D3
Helmsley 5 E4
Heriot 8 C2
Hermiston 25 D4
Herston 22 B4
Hetton-le-Hole 5 D2
Hexham 4 B1
High Blantyre 7 G2
High Blantyre 25 E3

High Etherley 4 C3
High Hawsker 5 F4
High Hesket 3 F2
High Lorton 3 E3
Hill End 12 C1
Hill of Fearn 16 A1
Hillend 25 E5
Hillington 25 D2
Hillside *Aber.* **24 C3**
Hillside *Angus* 13 E2
Hillside *Shet.* 23 E2
Hillswick 23 E2
Hinderwell 5 F3
Hirn 24 A2
Hollybush 7 E3
Holytown 25 F2
Holywood 3 D1
Hopeman 16 B2
Horden 5 D2
Hoswick 23 E4
Houbie 23 F1
Houghton le Spring 5 D2
Houndslow 9 D2
Houston 7 E2
Houton 22 B3
Howwood 7 F2
Huisinis 21 D3
Humbie 8 C2
Hunter's Quay 7 E1
Huntly 17 D3
Hurlford 7 F3
Hurworth-on-Tees 5 D3
Hutton Rudby 5 D4

I
Idrigil 14 B2
Inchbare 13 E2
Inchnadamph 18 B3
Inchture 13 D3
Ingleton 4 C3
Ingliston 25 D4
Innellan 7 D1
Innerleithen 8 C3
Insch 17 D3
Inveralligin 14 C2
Inverallochy 17 F2
Inveraray 11 E4
Inverarity 13 D3
Inverarnan 11 F4
Inverbervie 13 F1
Invercassley 18 C4
Invercharnan 11 E2
Inveresk 25 F4
Inverey 12 C1
Invergarry 15 E4
Invergordon 16 A2
Invergowrie 24 A4
Inverinan 11 E4
Inverkeilor 13 E2
Inverkeithing 8 B1
Inverkirkaig 18 A3
Inverlael 15 E1
Invermoriston 15 F4
Inverneil 6 C1
Inverness 16 A3
Inverness Airport 16 A2
Invernoaden 11 E4
Inverurie 17 E4
Irvine 7 E3
Isbister (Mainland)
   23 F2
Isle of Whithorn 2 C2

J
Jackton 25 D3
Jarrow 5 D1
Jedburgh 9 D3
Jemimaville 16 A2
John o' Groats 19 F1
Johnstone 7 F2
Johnstonebridge 8 B4
Joppa 25 F4
Juniper Green 25 D5

K
Kaimes 25 E5
Kames 6 D1
Keillmore 6 C1
Keiss 19 F1
Keith 17 D2
Kellas *Angus* 13 D3
Kellas *Angus* **24 B4**
Kellas *Moray* 16 C2
Kelso 9 D3
Kelty 12 C4
Kelvinside 25 D2
Kemnay 17 E4

Kemnay 24 A1
Kendal 4 A4
Kenknock 12 A3
Kenmore 12 B2
Kennacraig 6 C2
Kennethmont 17 D3
Kennoway 13 D4
Kensaleyre 14 B2
Kentallen 11 E2
Keoldale 18 B1
Keswick 3 F3
Kettletoft 22 C2
Kielder 9 D4
Kilberry 6 C2
Kilbirnie 7 E2
Kilcadzow 8 A2
Kilchattan 10 B4
Kilchenzie 6 C3
Kilchiaran 6 A3
Kilchoan 10 C2
Kilchoman 6 A3
Kilchrenan 11 E3
Kilconquhar 13 E4
Kilcreggan 7 E1
Kildonan Lodge 19 D3
Kildrummy 17 D4
Kilfinan 6 D1
Kilham 9 E3
Killean 6 C2
Killearn 7 F1
Killichonan 12 A2
Killiecrankie 12 B2
Killin 12 A3
Killingworth 5 D1
Killundine 10 C2
Kilmacolm 7 E1
Kilmalieu 11 D2
Kilmaluag 14 B2
Kilmany 24 A5
Kilmarnock 7 F3
Kilmartin 11 D4
Kilmaurs 7 E2
Kilmelford 11 D4
Kilmory *Arg. & B.* 6 C1
Kilmory *High.* 14 A4
Kilninian 10 B2
Kilninver 11 D3
Kiloran 10 B4
Kilrenny 13 E4
Kilsyth 7 G1
Kilwinning 7 E2
Kinbrace 19 D3
Kincardine 8 A1
Kincardine O'Neil 17 D4
Kincorth 24 C2
Kincraig 16 A4
Kinellar 24 B1
Kingarth 7 D2
Kinghorn 8 B1
Kinglassie 13 D4
Kingoodie 24 A5
Kingsbarns 13 E4
Kingsford 24 B2
Kingshouse 12 A3
Kingston 16 C2
Kingswells 24 B2
Kingussie 16 A4
Kinkell 25 E1
Kinloch 14 B4
Kinloch Hourn 15 D4
Kinloch Rannoch 12 A2
Kinlochard 12 A4
Kinlochbervie 18 B2
Kinlocheil 11 E1
Kinlochewe 15 D2
Kinlochleven 11 E2
Kinloss 16 B2
Kinmuck 24 B1
Kinross 12 C4
Kintore 17 E4
Kintore 24 A1
Kintour 6 B2
Kintra 6 A2
Kippen 12 A4
Kirk Michael 2 B4
Kirk Yetholm 9 E3
Kirkbean 3 D2
Kirkbride 3 E2
Kirkby Stephen 4 B4
Kirkbymoorside 5 E4
Kirkcaldy 8 B1
Kirkcolm 2 A1
Kirkconnel 7 G4
Kirkcowan 2 B2
Kirkcudbright 2 C2
Kirkinner 2 B2
Kirkintilloch 7 F1

Kirkintilloch 25 E1
Kirkliston 8 B1
Kirkliston 25 D4
Kirkmichael *P. & K.*
   12 C2
Kirkmichael *S.Ayr.* 7 E4
Kirkmuirhill 8 A2
Kirknewton *Northumb.*
   9 E3
Kirknewton *W.Loth.*
   8 B1
Kirknewton *W.Loth.*
   25 D5
Kirkoswald *Cumb.* 4 A2
Kirkoswald *S.Ayr.* 7 E4
Kirkpatrick Durham
   3 D1
Kirkpatrick-Fleming
   3 F1
Kirkton *Arg. & B.* 11 D4
Kirkton *Fife* **24 A5**
**Kirkton of Auchterhouse
   24 A4**
Kirkton of Culsalmond
   17 D3
Kirkton of Durris 13 F1
Kirkton of Durris 24 A3
Kirkton of Glenisla
   13 D2
Kirkton of Kingoldrum
   13 D2
**Kirkton of Maryculter
   24 B3**
Kirkton of Menmuir
   13 E2
**Kirkton of Monikie
   24 C4**
Kirkton of Skene 17 E4
Kirkton of Skene 24 B2
**Kirkton of Tealing
   24 B4**
Kirktown of Auchterless
   17 E3
Kirktown of Deskford
   17 D2
Kirkwall 22 B3
Kirriemuir 13 D2
Knayton 5 D4
Knightswood 25 D2
Knock 10 C3
Knockandhu 16 C4
Kyle of Lochalsh 14 C3
Kyleakin 14 C3
Kylerhea 14 C4
Kyles Scalpay 21 E3
Kylestrome 18 B2

L
Ladybank 13 D4
Ladykirk 9 E2
Ladysford 17 E2
Lagg 6 D3
Laggan (Invergarry) *High*
   11 F1
Laggan (Newtonmore)
   High. 12 A1
Lagganulva 10 C3
Laide 15 D1
Lairg 18 C4
Lamlash 6 D3
Lanark 8 A2
Lanchester 4 C2
Landerberry 24 A2
Langholm 3 F1
Langside 25 D2
Langwathby 4 A3
Larbert 8 A1
Largoward 13 D4
Largs 7 E2
Larkhall 7 G2
Larkhall 25 F3
Lasswade 25 F5
Latheron 19 E2
Latheronwheel 19 E3
Lauchintilly 24 A1
Lauder 8 C2
Laurencekirk 13 E2
Laurieston 2 C1
Law 8 A2
Lawers 12 A3
Laws 24 B4
Laxey 2 B4
Laxford Bridge 18 B2
Laxo 23 E2
Lazonby 4 A2
Leadburn 8 B2
Leadgate 4 C2

eadhills 8 A3
eckmelm 15 E1
edaig 11 D3
edmore 18 B3
eeming 5 D4
eith 8 B1
eith 25 E4
ennoxtown 7 F1
enzie 25 E1
eoch 24 A4
erwick 23 E3
esbury 9 F4
eschangie 24 A1
eslie 13 D4
esmahagow 8 A3
eswalt 2 A1
euchars 13 D3
euchars 24 B5
eumrabhagh 21 E3
even 13 D4
evenhall 25 F4
evenwick 23 E4
everburgh 21 D4
eyburn 4 C4
eylodge 24 A1
hanbryde 16 C2
ibberton 8 A2
iberton 25 E5
iff 24 A4
illiesleaf 8 C2
imekilnburn 25 F3
imekilns 8 B1
indores 13 D4
inksness 22 A3
inlithgow 8 A1
insidemore 15 F1
ittlemill *E.Ayr.* 7 F3
ittlemill *High.* 16 B2
ivingston 8 B1
oanhead 8 B2
oanhead 25 E5
oans 7 E3
och Baghasdail
 (Lochboisdale) 20 B3
och na Madadh
 (Lochmaddy) 20 B1
och Sgioport 20 B2
ochailort 11 D1
ochaline 10 C3
ochans 2 A2
ocharbriggs 3 E1
ochawe 11 E3
ochboisdale (Loch
 Baghasdail) 20 B3
ochcarron 15 D3
ochdon 11 D3
ochearnhead 12 A3
ochee 24 A4
ochend 15 F3
ochgelly 12 C4
ochgilphead 6 C1
ochgoilhead 11 F4
ochinver 18 A3
ochmaben 3 E1
ochmaddy (Loch na
 Madadh) 20 B1
ochranza 6 D2
ochwinnoch 7 E2
ockerbie 3 E1
ockton 5 F4
oftus 5 E3
ogan 7 F3
ogie 24 B5
ongbenton 5 D1
ongdrum 24 C1
ongforgan 13 D3
ongforgan 24 A5
ongframlington 9 F4
onghope 22 A4
onghorsley 9 F4
onghoughton 9 F3
ongmanhill 17 E2
ongmorn 16 C2
ongniddry 8 C1
ongside 17 F3
ongtown 3 F1
ossiemouth 16 C2
oth 22 C2
othmore 19 E3
ow Waters 25 F3
ower Diabaig 14 C2
ower Killeyan 6 A4
oweswater 3 E3
owick 9 E3
ucklawhill 24 B5
udag 20 A3
uggiebank 25 F1

Luib 14 B3
Lumphanan 17 D4
Luncarty 12 C3
Lundin Links 13 D4
Lunna 23 F2
Luss 7 F1
Lusta 14 A2
Lybster 19 F2
Lymekilns 25 E3
Lyne 24 A2
Lyne of Skene 17 E4
Lyne of Skene 24 A1
Lynemore 16 B3
Lynemouth 9 F4
Lyness 22 A4

M
Macduff 17 E2
Machan 25 F3
Macharioch 6 B3
Machrihanish 6 B3
Macmerry 8 C1
Maidens 7 E4
**Mains of Ardestie
 24 C4**
Mains of Drum 24 B2
Mains of Linton 24 A1
Mallaig 10 C1
Malleny Mills 25 D5
Malletsheugh 25 D3
Mannofield 24 C2
Markinch 13 D4
Marske-by-the-Sea 5 E3
Marybank 15 F3
Maryhill 25 D2
Marykirk 13 E2
Marypark 16 C3
Maryport 3 E2
Marywell (Portlethen)
 Aber. 24 C3
Marywell (Deeside) *Aber.*
 13 E1
Mastrick 24 C2
Mauchline 7 F3
Maud 17 F3
Maughold 2 C4
Maybole 7 E4
Mayfield 25 F5
Mealsgate 3 E2
Mearns 25 D3
Meigle 13 D3
Meikle Earnock 25 F3
Meikle Kilmory 7 D2
Meikleour 12 C3
Melmerby 4 A2
Melrose 8 C3
Melsonby 4 C4
Melvaig 14 C1
Melvich 19 D1
Memsie 17 F2
Menstrie 12 B4
Methlick 17 E3
Methven 12 C3
Mey 19 F1
Miavaig 21 D2
Mickleton 4 B3
Mid Ardlaw 17 F2
Mid Yell 23 F1
Midbea 22 B3
Middleham 4 C4
Middlesbrough 5 D3
Middleton 24 B1
Middleton of Potterton
 24 C1
Middleton Park 24 C1
Middleton-in-Teesdale
 4 B3
Midlem 8 C3
Milfield 9 E3
Mill of Monquich 24 B3
Millden 24 C1
Millerhill 25 F5
Millhouse 6 D1
Millport 7 D2
Milltimber 24 B2
Milltown of Rothiemay
 17 D3
Milnathort 12 C4
Milngavie 7 F1
Milngavie 25 D1
Milovaig 14 A2
Milton (Strathconon)
 High. 15 E2
Milton (Drumnadrochit)
 High. 15 F3
Milton *P. & K.* 12 B3
Milton Bridge 25 E5

Milton of Campsie 7 F1
**Milton of Campsie
 25 E1**
**Milton of Cullerlie
 24 A2**
Minard 11 E4
Minnigaff 2 B1
Mintlaw 17 F3
Moffat 8 B4
Mollinsburn 25 F1
Moniaive 7 G4
Monifieth 13 E3
Monifieth 24 C4
Monikie 24 C4
Monimail 13 D4
Monreith 2 B2
Montrose 13 E2
Moodiesburn 25 E1
Morar 10 C1
Morebattle 9 D3
Morenish 12 A3
Moresby 3 E3
Morningside 25 E4
Morpeth 4 C1
Moscow 7 F3
Mossat 17 D4
Mossbank 23 E2
Mossblown 7 F3
Mossend 25 F2
Mosstodloch 16 C2
Motherwell 7 G2
Motherwell 25 F3
Mountbenger 8 C3
Moy 16 A3
Muchalls 13 F1
Mugdock 25 D1
Muir of Fowlis 17 D4
Muir of Ord 15 F2
Muirdrum 13 E3
Muirdrum 24 C4
Muirhead *Angus* 13 D3
Muirhead *Angus* 24 A4
Muirhead *N.Lan.* 25 E2
Muirkirk 7 G3
Mulben 16 C2
Mundurno 24 C1
Munlochy 16 A2
Murroes 24 B4
Murton 5 D2
Musselburgh 8 C1
Musselburgh 25 F4
Muthill 12 B4
Mybster 19 E2
Myrebird 24 A3

N
Nairn 16 A2
Nateby 4 B4
Near Sawrey 3 F4
Neilston 7 F2
Nenthead 4 B2
Nerston 25 E3
Netherley 13 F1
Netherley 24 B3
Netherton *N.Lan.* 25 F3
Netherton *Northumb.*
 9 E4
Nethy Bridge 16 B4
New Abbey 3 D1
New Aberdour 17 E2
New Byth 17 E2
New Cumnock 7 F4
New Deer 17 E3
New Galloway 2 C1
New Leeds 17 F2
New Luce 2 A1
New Pitsligo 17 E2
Newarthill 25 F3
Newbattle 25 F5
Newbiggin-by-the-Sea
 5 D1
Newbigging (West)
 Angus 24 B4
Newbigging (East)
 Angus 24 B4
Newbigging *S. Lan.* 8 A2
Newbridge 25 D4
Newburgh *Aber.* 17 F3
Newburgh *Fife* 13 D4
Newburn 4 C1
Newby Bridge 3 F4
Newcastle International
 Airport 4 C1
Newcastle upon Tyne
 4 C1
Newcastleton 3 F1
Newcraighall 25 F4

Newington 25 E4
Newlandrig 25 F5
Newmachar 17 E4
Newmachar 24 B1
Newmains 8 A2
Newmarket 21 F2
Newmill 17 D2
Newmilns 7 F3
Newport 19 E3
Newport-on-Tay 13 D3
Newport-on-Tay 24 B5
Newton 11 E4
Newton Aycliffe 5 D3
Newton Mearns 7 F2
Newton Mearns 25 D3
**Newton of Affleck
 24 B4**
Newton Stewart 2 B1
Newtongrange 25 F5
Newtonhill 13 F1
Newtonhill 24 C3
Newtonmore 16 A4
Newtown St. Boswells
 9 D3
Newtyle 13 D3
Niddrie 25 E4
Nigg 24 C2
Ninemile Bar
 (Crocketford) 3 D1
Nisbet 9 D3
Nitshill 25 D2
Norham 9 E2
North Ballachulish
 11 E2
North Berwick 8 C1
North Cowton 5 D4
North Dell 21 F1
North Kessock 16 A3
North Middleton 8 C1
North Queensferry 8 B1
North Roe 23 E2
North Shields 5 D1
North Sunderland 9 F3
North Tarbothill 24 C1
Northallerton 5 D4
Northfield 24 C2
Northton 21 D3

O
Oakley 8 A1
Oban 11 E3
Ochiltree 7 F3
Ockle 10 C2
Oddsta 23 F1
Old Aberdeen 24 C2
Old Dailly 7 E4
Old Kinnernie 24 A2
Oldmeldrum 17 E3
Olgrinmore 19 E2
Ollaberry 23 E2
Onich 11 E2
Ormiston 8 C1
Orphir 22 B3
Orrok House 24 C1
Orton 4 A4
Oskaig 14 B3
Otter Ferry 6 D1
Otterburn 9 E4
Otterswick 23 F2
Overbister 22 C2
**Overton *Aberdeen*
 24 B1**
Overton *Aber.* 24 A1
Overtown 8 A2
Oxnam 9 D3
Oxton 8 C2
Oykel Bridge 15 F1

P
Paisley 7 F2
Palnackie 3 D2
Panbride 24 C4
Parkgate 3 E1
Parkhead 25 E2
Partick 25 D2
Parton 3 D3
Path of Condie 12 C4
Pathhead 25 F5
Patna 7 E4
Patterdale 3 F3
Paxton 9 E2
Peebles 8 B3
Peel 2 B4
Pegswood 4 C1
Peinchorran 14 B3
Pencaitland 8 C1

Penicuik 8 B2
Penicuik 25 E5
Peninver 6 C3
Pennyghael 10 C3
Penpont 8 A4
Penrith 4 A3
Perth 12 C3
Peterculter 17 E4
Peterculter 24 B2
Peterhead 17 F3
Peterlee 5 D2
Pickering 5 F4
Pickletillem 24 B5
Pierowall 22 B2
Pinwherry 2 A1
Pirnmill 6 C2
Pitagowan 12 B2
Pitlochry 12 B2
Pitmedden 17 E3
Pitscottie 13 D4
Pittentrail 19 D4
Pittenweem 13 E4
Plains 25 F2
Plean 8 A1
Polbeth 8 A2
Polloch 11 D2
Pollok 25 D2
Pollokshaws 25 D2
Pollokshields 25 D2
Polmont 8 A1
Polnoon 25 D3
Polton 25 E5
Polwarth 9 D2
Ponteland 4 C1
Poolewe 14 C1
Pooley Bridge 3 F3
Port Appin 11 D3
Port Askaig 6 B2
Port Bannatyne 7 D2
Port Driseach 6 D1
Port Ellen 6 A2
Port Elphinstone 24 A1
Port Glasgow 7 E1
Port Henderson 14 C2
Port Logan 2 A2
Port nan Long 20 B1
Port of Menteith 12 A4
Port of Ness 21 F1
Port William 2 B2
Portencross 7 E2
Portknockie 17 D2
Portlethen 13 F1
Portlethen 24 C3
**Portlethen Village
 24 C3**
Portmahomack 16 B1
Portnacon 18 B1
Portnacroish 11 D2
Portnaguran 21 F2
Portnahaven 6 A4
Portnalong 14 A3
Portobello 25 F4
Portpatrick 2 A2
Portree 14 B3
Portsoy 17 D2
Potterton 24 C1
Powburn 9 F3
Powmill 12 C4
Preston 9 D2
Prestonpans 8 C1
Prestonpans 25 F4
Prestwick 7 E3
Prestwick (Glasgow)
 International Airport
 7 E3
Prudhoe 4 C2

Q
Quarff 23 E4
Quarter 25 F3
Queensferry (South
 Queensferry) 8 B1
**Queensferry (South
 Queensferry) 25 D4**

R
Rafford 16 B2
Rait 13 D3
Ramsey 2 B4
Rathillet 13 D3
Rathillet 24 A5
Ratho 8 B1
Ratho 25 D4
Ratho Station 25 D4
Rattray 12 C3
Ravenglass 3 E4
Rawyards 25 F2

Reay 19 D1
Red Point 14 C2
Redcar 5 E3
Redcastle 15 F3
Redford 13 E3
Redhill 24 A2
Reiff 18 A3
Reiss 19 F2
Renfrew 25 D2
Rennington 9 F3
Rescobie 13 E2
Reston 9 E2
Rhiconich 18 B2
Rhu 7 E1
Rhynie 17 D3
Richmond 4 C4
Rickarton 13 F1
Riding Mill 4 C2
Riggend 25 F2
Rigside 8 A3
Ringford 2 C2
Roadside 19 E1
Roadside of Kinneff
   13 F1
Roberton *Sc.Bord.* 8 C4
Roberton *S.Lan.* 8 A3
Robin Hood's Bay 5 F4
Rochester 9 E4
Rockcliffe 3 D2
Rodel 21 D4
Rogart 19 D4
Romannobridge 8 B2
Rosedale Abbey 5 E4
Rosehearty 17 F2
Rosemarkie 16 A2
Rosewell 8 B2
Rosewell 25 E5
Roshven 11 D1
Roskhill 14 A3
Roslin 8 B2
Roslin 25 E5
Rothbury 9 E4
Rothes 16 C3
Rothesay 7 D2
Rothiesholm 22 C2
Rowlands Gill 4 C2
Roybridge 11 F1
Rutherend 25 E3
Rutherglen 7 F2
Rutherglen 25 E2
Ruthrieston 24 C2

S

Sacriston 4 C2
Saddell 6 C3
Saighdinis 20 B1
St. Abbs 9 E1
St. Andrews 13 E4
St. Bees 3 D3
St. Combs 17 F2
St. Cyrus 13 E2
St. Fergus 17 F2
St. Fillans 12 A3
St. John's Chapel 4 B2
St. John's Town of Dalry
   2 C1
St. Margaret's Hope
   22 B4
St. Mary's 22 B3
St. Michaels 24 B5
St. Monans 13 E4
Salen *Arg. & B.* 10 C3
Salen *High.* 11 D2
Saline 8 A1
Salmond's Muir 24 C4
Salsburgh 8 A2
Saltburn-by-the-Sea
   5 E3
Saltcoats 7 E2
Sanaigmore 6 A3
Sandgarth 22 B3
Sandhead 2 A2
Sandness 23 D3
Sandsend 5 F3
Sandwick 23 E4
Sandygate 2 B4
Sanquhar 7 G4
Satley 4 C2
Scalasaig 10 B4
Scalby 5 F4
Scalloway 23 E3
Scapa 22 B3
Scarborough 5 F4
Scardroy 15 E2
Scarinish 10 A3
Scone 12 C3

Sconser 14 B3
Scorton 4 C4
Scotch Corner 4 C4
Scotstoun 25 D2
Scotton 4 C4
Scourie 18 A2
Scousburgh 23 E4
Scrabster 19 E1
Scremerston 9 E2
Seaham 5 D2
Seahouses 9 F3
Seamill 7 E2
Seascale 3 E4
Seaton 3 E3
Seaton Delaval 5 D1
Seaton Sluice 5 D1
Sedbergh 4 A4
Sedgefield 5 D3
Seghill 5 D1
Selkirk 8 C3
Sellafield 3 E4
Sellafirth 23 F1
Setter 23 E3
Sgiogarstaigh 21 F1
Shap 4 A3
Shawbost 21 E1
Sherburn 5 D2
Shettleston 25 E2
Shiel Bridge 15 D4
Shieldaig 14 C2
Shilbottle 9 F4
Shildon 4 C3
Shinness Lodge 18 C3
Shiremoor 5 D1
Shotts 8 A2
Silloth 3 E2
Silverburn 25 E5
Siulaisiadar 21 F2
Skaill (West Coast) *Ork.*
   22 A3
Skaill (East Coast) *Ork.*
   22 C3
Skaw 23 F2
Skeld 23 E3
Skelmorlie 7 E1
Skelton 5 E3
Skelwick 22 B2
Skerray 18 C1
Skipness 6 C2
Slamannan 8 A1
Sleights 5 F4
Sligachan 14 B3
Smailholm 9 D3
Sollas 20 B1
Sorbie 2 B2
Sorisdale 10 B2
Sorn 7 F3
South Bank 5 E3
South Gyle 25 D4
South Hetton 5 D2
South Kirkton 24 A2
South Queensferry
   (Queensferry) 8 B1
**South Queensferry
   (Queensferry) 25 D4**
South Shields 5 D1
Southdean 9 D4
Southend 6 C4
Spean Bridge 11 F1
Spennymoor 5 D3
Spey Bay 16 C2
Spinningdale 16 A1
Spittal 19 E2
Spittal of Glenshee
   12 C2
Springburn 25 E2
Springholm 3 D1
Springside 7 E3
Staffin 14 B2
Staindrop 4 C3
Staintondale 5 F4
Stalling Busk 4 B4
Stamfordham 4 C1
Stand 25 F2
Stane 8 A2
Stanhope 4 B2
Stanley *Dur.* 4 C2
Stanley *P. & K.* 12 C3
Stannington 4 C1
Startforth 4 C3
Stenhousemuir 8 A1
Stenness 23 D2
Stenton 9 D1
Steornabhagh
   (Stornoway) 21 F2
Stepps 25 E2
Stevenston 7 E2

Stewarton 7 E2
Stichill 9 D3
Stilligarry 20 A2
Stirling 12 B4
Stobo 8 B3
Stocksfield 4 C2
Stockton-on-Tees 5 D3
Stoer 18 A3
Stokesley 5 E4
Stonehaven 13 F1
Stonehouse 7 G2
Stoneykirk 2 A2
Stoneywood 24 B1
Stonybreck 23 D4
Stornoway
   (Steornabhagh) 21 F2
Stow 8 C2
Strachan 13 E1
Strachur 11 E4
Straiton 25 E5
Straloch 12 C2
Stranraer 2 A2
Strathaven 7 G2
Strathblane 7 F1
Strathdon 16 C4
Strathmiglo 12 C4
Strathpeffer 15 F2
Strathy 19 D1
Strathyre 12 A4
Strichen 17 F2
Stromeferry 14 C3
Stromness 22 A3
Stronachlachar 11 F4
Strone 7 E1
Strontian 11 D2
Stuartfield 17 F3
Sumburgh 23 E4
Sunderland 5 D2
Sunnyside 24 B3
Swanston 25 E5
Swinton 9 E2
Symbister 23 F3
Symington *S.Ayr.* 7 E3
Symington *S.Lan.* 8 A3
Syre 18 C2

T

Tain 16 A1
Talisker 14 A3
Talladale 15 D2
Talmine 18 C1
Tannadice 13 E2
Tannochside 25 E2
Tarbert (Kintyre) *Arg. & B.*
   6 C1
Tarbert (Jura) *Arg. & B.*
   6 B1
Tarbert (An Tairbeart)
   W.Isles 21 E3
Tarbet 11 F4
Tarbolton 7 F3
Tarfside 13 E1
Tarrel 16 B1
Tarves 17 E3
Tavelty 24 A1
Tayinloan 6 C2
Taynuilt 11 E3
Tayport 13 D3
Tayport 24 B5
Tayvallich 6 C1
Tealing 13 D3
Tealing 24 B4
Teangue 14 C4
Tebay 4 A4
Temple Sowerby 4 A3
Teviothead 8 C4
Thainstone 24 A1
The Birks 24 A2
The Murray 25 E3
The Neuk 24 A3
Thornaby-on-Tees 5 D3
Thornhill *D. & G.* 8 A4
Thornhill *Stir.* 12 A4
Thornley 5 D2
Thornliebank 25 D3
Thornton 13 D4
Thorntonhall 25 D3
Threlkeld 3 F3
Thriepley 24 A4
Thropton 9 E4
Thrumster 19 F2
Thursby 3 F2
Thurso 19 E1
Thwaite 4 B4
Tibbermore 12 C3
Tighnabruaich 6 D1
Tillicoultry 12 B4

Tillyfourie 17 D4
Timsgearraidh 21 D2
Tingwall 22 B3
Toab 23 E4
Tobermory 10 C2
Toberonochy 11 D4
Todhills 24 B4
Toft 23 E2
Togston 9 F4
Tolastadh a'Chaolais
   21 E2
Tolastadh Úr 21 F1
Toll of Birness 17 F3
Tollcross 25 E2
Tomatin 16 A3
Tomich 16 A2
Tomintoul 16 C4
Tomnavoulin 16 C3
Tongland 15 D2
Tongue 18 C2
Tore 15 F2
Tormore 6 C3
Torphichen 8 A1
Torphins 17 D4
Torrance 7 F1
Torrance 25 E1
Torrance House 25 E3
Torridon 15 D2
Torrin 14 B4
Torry 24 C2
Torthorwald 3 E1
Torver 3 F4
Toscaig 14 C3
Tow Law 4 C2
Town Yetholm 9 E3
Townhead of Greenlaw
   3 D1
Tranent 8 C1
Tressait 12 B2
Trimdon 5 D3
Trinity *Angus* 13 E2
Trinity *Edin.* 25 E4
Trochry 12 C3
Troon 7 E3
Trottick 24 B4
Troutbeck 3 F4
Troutbeck Bridge 3 F4
Tummel Bridge 12 B2
Tunga 21 F2
Turnberry 7 E4
Turriff 17 E2
Twatt 22 A2
Twechar 7 G1
Twechar 25 F1
Tweedmouth 9 E2
Tweedsmuir 8 B3
Twynholm 2 C2
Tyndrum 11 F3
Tynemouth 5 D1

U

Uachdar 20 B2
Uddingston 7 G2
Uddingston 25 E2
Uddington 8 A3
Udston 25 F3
Uig 14 B2
Ulbster 19 F2
Ulgham 9 F4
Ullapool 15 D1
Ulpha 3 E4
Ulsta 23 E2
Unapool 18 B2
Upper Burnhaugh 24 B3
Upper Knockando 16 C3
Upper Muirskie 24 B3
Upper Victoria 24 C4
Urafirth 23 E2
Ushaw Moor 4 C2
Uyeasound 23 F1

V

Valsgarth 23 F1
Veensgarth 23 E3
Vidlin 23 F2
Viewpark 25 F2
Voe 23 E2

W

Walls 23 E3
Wallsend 5 D1
Wallyford 25 F4
Warcop 4 A3
Wark 4 B1
Warkworth 9 F4
Warwick Bridge 3 F2
Wasbister 22 B2

Washington 5 D2
Watchgate 4 A4
Waterbeck 3 F1
Waterfoot 25 D3
Waterside 25 E1
Watten 19 F2
Wattston 25 F2
Weem 12 B2
Weisdale 23 E3
Wellbank 24 B2
Wemyss Bay 7 E1
Wensley 4 C4
West Auckland 4 C3
West Calder 8 A2
West Kilbride 7 E2
West Linton 8 B2
West Park 24 A3
West Sandwick 23 E1
West Tarbert 6 C1
West Yell 23 E2
Wester Fintray 24 B1
Wester Hailes 25 E5
Wester Ord 24 B2
Westerdale 19 E2
Westfield 25 F1
Westgate 4 B2
Westhill 17 E4
Westhill 24 B2
Westness 22 B2
Westnewton 3 E2
Westruther 9 D2
Westside 24 B3
Westwood 25 E3
Wetheral 3 F2
Whalton 4 C1
Whauphill 2 B2
Wheatley Hill 5 D2
Whickham 4 C2
Whifflet 25 F2
Whitburn 8 A2
Whitby 5 F3
Whitecairns 24 C1
Whitecraig 8 C1
Whitecraig 25 F4
Whitehall 22 C2
Whitehaven 3 D3
Whitehill 25 F5
Whitehills 17 E2
Whiteness 23 E3
Whiterashes 17 E4
Whithorn 2 B2
Whiting Bay 6 D3
Whitley Bay 5 D1
Whittingham 9 E4
Wick 19 F2
Wigton 3 F2
Wigtown 2 B2
Wilkieston 25 D5
Willington 4 C3
Winchburgh 8 B1
Windermere 3 F4
Windygates 13 D4
Wingate 5 D2
Winston 4 C3
Winton 4 B3
Wishaw 8 A2
Witton Gilbert 4 C2
Wolsingham 4 C2
Woodhaven 24 B5
Woodland 4 C3
Woodside 24 C2
Wooler 9 E3
Workington 3 E3
Wormit 13 D3
Wormit 24 A5
Wrelton 5 F4

Y

Yarm 5 D3
Yarrow 8 C3
Yetts o' Muckhart 12 C4
Yoker 25 D2

Key to map symbols

M74 Motorway / under construction or proposed

A82 Primary road dual / single

A70 'A' Road dual / single

B793 'B' Road dual / single

Other road dual / single

Toll One-way street / Toll

Restricted access / Pedestrian street

Minor road / Track

FB Footpath / Cycle path / Footbridge

Railway line / station

Railway tunnel / Level crossing

Ⓢ Subway / Bus (Coach) station

Ⓟ Car Park

Leisure / Tourism

Shopping / Retail

Administration / Law

Education

Hospital

Industry / Commerce

Notable building

Health centre

Pol PO Lib Police station / Post Office / Library

✝ ☾ ✡ Church / Mosque / Synagogue

🎦 🎭 Cinema / Theatre

⊠ Hilton Major Hotel

ℹ ℹ Tourist information centre (all year / seasonal)

Fire station / Ambulance station / Community centre

Abbreviations used in town plan indexes

All	Alley
App	Approach
Arc	Arcade
Av	Avenue
Bk	Bank
Bldgs	Buildings
Boul	Boulevard
Bri	Bridge
Cen	Central/Centre
Cft	Croft
Ch	Church
Circ	Circus
Clo	Close
Coll	College
Cor	Corner
Cotts	Cottages
Cres	Crescent
Ct	Court
Dr	Drive
E	East
Esp	Esplanade
Est	Estate
Ex	Exchange
Fm	Farm
Gdn	Garden
Gdns	Gardens
Gra	Grange
Grn	Green
Gro	Grove
Hts	Heights
Ho	House
Hos	Hospital
Ind	Industrial
Junct	Junction
La	Lane
Ln	Loan
Mans	Mansion
Mkt	Market
Ms	Mews
Mt	Mount
N	North
Par	Parade
Pk	Park
Pl	Place
Quad	Quadrant
Rd	Road
Ri	Rise
S	South
Sch	School
Sq	Square
St	Street
St.	Saint
Sta	Station
Ter	Terrace
Twr	Tower
Vills	Villas
Vw	View
W	West
Wd	Wood
Wds	Woods
Wf	Wharf
Wk	Walk
Wks	Works
Yd	Yard

ABERDEEN

Maps 32-35   Index 36-37
Scale 4 inches to 1 mile

DUNDEE

Maps 38-39   Index 40-41
Scale 4.6 inches to 1 mile

EDINBURGH

Maps 42-51   Index 52-57
Scale 4 inches to 1 mile
City centre map 5.7 inches to 1 mile

GLASGOW

Maps 58-65   Index 66-72
Scale 4 inches to 1 mile

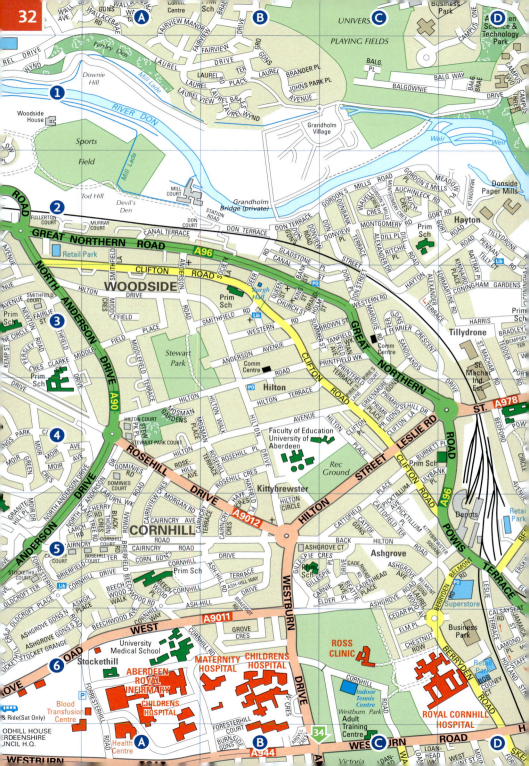

A

Street	Ref
Abbey La	35 H4
Abbey Pl	35 H4
Abbey Rd	35 H4
Abbey Sq	35 H4
Abbotsford La	35 H4
Abergeldie Rd	34 C5
Abergeldie Ter	34 C5
Academy St	35 E3
Advocates Rd	33 F6
Albert La	34 B3
Albert Pl	34 C2
Albert Quay	35 G3
Albert St	34 C2
Albert Ter	34 C3
Albury Pl	35 E4
Albury Rd	34 D4
Albyn Gro	34 C3
Albyn La	34 C3
Albyn Pl	34 C3
Albyn Ter	34 C3
Alexander Dr	32 C2
Alexander Ter	32 C2
Allan St	34 C4
Allenvale Gdns	34 D6
Allenvale Rd	34 D6
Anderson Av	32 B3
Anderson Rd	32 A2
Annfield Ter	34 B4
Ann St	34 D1
Ardarroch Pl	33 G5
Ardarroch Rd	33 F5
Argyll Cres	34 B1
Argyll Pl	34 B1
Ashgrove Av	32 C5
Ashgrove Ct	32 B5
Ashgrove Rd	32 B3
Ash-hill Dr	32 A5
Ash-hill Rd	32 B5
Ash-hill Way	32 B5
Ashley Gdns	34 B4
Ashley Gro	34 C4
Ashley La	34 B4
Ashley Pk Dr	34 B4
Ashley Pk La	34 C4
Ashley Pk N	34 C4
Ashley Pk S	34 C4
Ashley Rd	34 C4
Ashvale Pl	34 C3
Auchinleck Cres	32 C2
Auchinleck Rd	32 C2
Aulton Ct	33 G3

B

Street	Ref
Back Hilton Rd	32 C5
Back Wynd	34 D1
Baker St	34 D1
Balgownie Brae	33 F3
Balgownie Ct	33 F3
Balgownie Cres	33 F1
Balgownie Dr	32 C1
Balgownie Gdns	32 D1
Balgownie Pl	32 D1
Balgownie Rd	33 F1
Balgownie Way	32 C1
Balmoral Ct	34 C5
Balmoral Pl	34 C5
Balmoral Rd	34 D5
Balmoral Ter	34 C5
Balnagask Rd	35 H5
Baltic Pl	35 H2
Baltic St	35 G2
Bank St	35 E4
Bank St (Woodside)	32 B3
Battock Pl	35 G5
Baxter St	35 H4
Bayview Ct	33 G4
Bayview Rd	34 A3
Bayview Rd S	34 A4
Beach Boul	35 G1
Beachview Ct	34 A3
Beaconsfield Pl	34 A3
Beattie Av	32 C5
Bedford Av	32 D4
Bedford Pl	32 D5
Bedford Rd	32 D5
Beechgrove Av	34 B1
Beechgrove Gdns	34 B1
Beechgrove Pl	34 B2
Beechgrove Ter	34 B2
Beechwood Av	32 A6
Beechwood Pl	32 A5
Beechwood Rd	32 A5
Beechwood Wk	32 A5
Belgrave Ter	34 C2
Belmont Gdns	32 C5
Belmont Rd	32 D5
Belmont St	35 E2
Belvidere Cres	34 C2
Belvidere St	34 C1
Berryden Rd	32 D6
Berry St	35 F1
Bethany Gdns	34 D4
Blackfriars St	35 E1
Blacks La	35 G3
Blackthorn Cres	32 A5
Blaikies Quay	35 G3
Blenheim La	34 B2
Blenheim Pl	34 B2
Bloomfield Ct	34 D5
Bloomfield Pl	34 D4
Bloomfield Rd	34 D5
Bob Cooney Ct	32 D6
Boddie Pl	33 F6
Bon Accord Cres	35 E3
Bon Accord St	35 E3
Bonnymuir Pl	34 B1
Bradley Ter	32 D3
Braefoot Rd	32 B5
Braemar Pl	34 C5
Brander Pl	32 B1
Bridge of Don	33 G2
Bridge St	35 E2
Brierfield Rd	32 A5
Brighton Pl	34 B4
Bright St	35 E5
Brig o' Balgownie	33 F1
Brimmond Pl	34 C6
Broomhill Av	34 C6
Broomhill Ct	34 C5
Broomhill Pl	34 C5
Broomhill Rd	34 C5
Broomhill Ter	34 C6
Brown St	32 C3
Brunswick Pl	35 H5
Burnbank Pl	35 H5
Burnbank Ter	35 H5
Burnett Pl	32 C4
Burns Gdns	34 B1
Burnside Gdns	34 B1
Burns Rd	34 A4

C

Street	Ref
Cadenhead Pl	32 C5
Cadenhead Rd	32 C5
Cairnaquheen Gdns	34 A1
Cairncry Av	32 A5
Cairncry Cres	32 B5
Cairncry Rd	32 A5
Cairncry Ter	32 A5
Cairnfield Pl	34 B1
Cairnfold Rd	33 E1
Cairnview Cres	32 A5
Caledonian Pl	35 E4
Calsayseat Rd	32 D6
Camperdown Rd	34 A1
Campus One	32 D1
Campus Three	32 D1
Campus Two	32 D1
Canal Pl	33 E6
Canal Rd	33 E6
Canal St	33 E6
Canal St (Woodside)	32 B2
Canal Ter	32 A2
Carden Pl	34 B3
Carden Ter	34 C3
Carlton Pl	34 A2
Carnie Dr	32 B5
Castle Ter	35 G2
Catherine St	35 E1
Cattofield Gdns	32 C5
Cattofield Pl	32 C5
Cattofield Ter	32 C5
Causewayend	33 E6
Cedar Pl	32 C6
Chanonry	33 E3
Chapel St	34 D2
Charles St	33 E6
Charlotte Gdns	35 E1
Charlotte St	35 E1
Chattan Pl	34 C4
Cherry Rd	32 A5
Chestnut Row	32 C6
Cheyne Rd	33 F3
Church St	35 G2
Church St (Woodside)	32 B3
Claremont Gdns	34 C4
Claremont Gro	34 C4
Claremont Pl	34 C4
Claremont St	34 C4
Clarence St	35 G2
Clarks La	33 F3
Clifton La	32 C4
Clifton Pl	32 C4
Clifton Rd	32 A3
Clyde St	35 G3
College Bounds	33 E4
College St	35 E3
Colville Pl	33 F6
Commerce St	35 G2
Commercial Quay	35 G3
Coningham Gdns	32 D3
Coningham Rd	32 D3
Coningham Ter	32 D3
Constitution St	35 G1
Cornhill Ct	32 A5
Cornhill Dr	32 A5
Cornhill Gdns	32 A5
Cornhill Rd	32 A6
Cornhill Ter	32 A5
Cornhill Way	32 A6
Corsehill Gdns	32 D1
Corunna Rd	33 G1
Cottage Brae	34 C4
Cotton St	35 G1
Cottown of Balgownie	33 F1
Coull Gdns	33 E1
Craigielea Av	34 A5
Craigie Loanings	34 C2
Craigie Pk	34 C2
Craigie St	35 E1
Craigton Ct	34 A6
Cranford Pl	34 B6
Cranford Rd	34 A6
Cranford Ter	34 A6
Crathie Gdns W	34 D6
Crathie Ter	34 C6
Crimon Pl	35 E2
Crombie Pl	35 G4
Crombie Rd	35 G4
Cromwell Gdns	34 A4
Cromwell Rd	34 A4
Crooked La	35 E1
Crown St	35 E3
Crown Ter	35 E3

D

Street	Ref
Danestone Pl	33 F1
Danestone Ter	33 F1
Davan Pk	33 E1
Deemount Av	35 E5
Deemount Gdns	35 E5
Deemount Rd	35 E5
Deemount Ter	35 E5
Dee Pl	35 E3
Deer Rd	32 B3
Dee St	35 E3
Dempsey Ter	32 D3
Denburn Rd	35 E1
Denmore Gdns	33 E1
Desswood Pl	34 B3
Devanha Cres	35 E4
Devanha Gdns	35 E4
Devanha Gdns E	35 E4
Devanha Gdns S	35 E4
Devanha Gdns W	35 E4
Devanha Ter	35 E4
Devonshire Rd	34 B4
Diamond St	35 E2
Dill Pl	32 C2
Dill Rd	32 C2
Dominies Ct	32 A4
Dominies Rd	32 A4
Donbank Ter	32 B2
Don Ct	32 A2
Don Gdns	32 B2
Donmouth Ct	33 G1
Donmouth Cres	33 G1
Donmouth Gdns	33 G1
Donmouth Rd	33 G1
Donmouth Ter	33 G1
Don Pl	32 C3
Don St (Old Aberdeen)	33 E3
Don St (Woodside)	32 C3
Don Ter	32 B2
Donview Ho	33 G3
Donview Pl	32 C2
Donview Rd	32 B2
Downies Brae	35 G5
Downies Pl	35 H5
Duff St	35 G1
Dunbar St	33 E4
Duthie Pl	34 A6
Duthie Ter	34 A6

E

Street	Ref
East N St	35 F1
East Tullos Ind Est	35 H6
Elder Pl	32 B5
Elmbank Rd	33 E6
Elmbank Ter	32 D5
Elmfield Av	32 D5
Elmfield Pl	32 D5
Elmfield Ter	32 D5
Elm Pl	32 C6
Elphinstone Rd	33 E4
Errol Pl	33 F6
Errol St	33 F6
Erskine St	32 D5
Esplanade	35 H2
Esslemont Av	34 C1
Exchange St	35 F2

F

Street	Ref
Fairview Brae	32 A1
Fairview Dr	32 B1
Farmers Hall La	34 D1
Farquhar Av	35 H5
Farquhar Brae	35 H5
Farquhar Rd	35 H5
Fernie Brae	35 G6
Ferrier Cres	32 C3
Ferrier Gdns	32 C3
Ferryhill Gdns	35 E4
Ferryhill La	35 E4
Ferryhill Pl	35 E4
Ferryhill Rd	35 E4
Ferryhill Ter	35 E4
Ferry Pl	35 H3
Firhill Rd	33 E5
Fish St	35 G2
Fonthill Gdns E	34 D5
Fonthill Gdns W	34 D4
Fonthill Rd	34 D4
Fonthill Ter	34 D4
Forbesfield La	34 B4
Forbesfield Rd	34 B4
Forbes St	34 D1
Forest Av	34 B4
Forest Av La	34 B4
Foresterhill Ct	34 B1
Forestgait	34 A2
Forest Rd	34 A2
Formartine Rd	32 C3
Forresterhill Rd	32 A6
Fountainhall Rd	34 B2
Fowlershill Gdns	33 E1
Fraser Ct	33 E6
Fraserfield Gdns	33 F1
Fraser Pl	32 D6
Fraser Rd	32 D6
Fraser St	32 D6
Frederick St	35 F1
Froghall Av	33 E6
Froghall Gdns	33 E6
Froghall Pl	33 E5
Froghall Rd	33 E6
Froghall Ter	33 E6
Froghall Vw	33 E5

G

Street	Ref
Gairn Circle	34 D5
Gairn Ct	34 D5
Gairn Cres	34 D5
Gairn Rd	34 D5
Gairn Ter	34 D5
Gallowgate	35 F1
Garvock Wynd	35 H2
George St	33 E6
Gerrard St	35 E1
Gilcomston Steps	34 D1
Gillespie Cres	32 B5
Gillespie Pl	32 B5
Girdleness Rd	35 H5
Girdleness Ter	35 G6
Girdlestone Pl	35 H5
Gladstone Pl	34 B3
Gladstone Pl (Woodside)	32 B2
Glenbervie Rd	35 G4
Golf Rd	33 G5
Gordondale Ct	34 A2
Gordondale Rd	34 B1
Gordon La	34 A6
Gordon's Mills Cres	32 C2
Gordon's Mills Pl	32 C2
Gordon's Mills Rd	32 C2
Gordon St	35 E3
Gort Rd	32 C2
Grampian La	35 G4
Grampian Pl	35 F5
Grampian Rd	35 G4
Grandholm Br (Private)	32 B2
Grandholm St	32 B3
Granton Pl	34 C3
Granville Pl	34 B5
Gray St	34 B5
Gray St Ms	34 B5
Great Northern Rd	32 C3
Great Southern Rd	34 D5
Great Western Pl	34 C5
Great Western Rd	34 A5
Greenmore Gdns	32 C4
Greenwell Pl	35 H6
Greenwell Rd	35 H6
Gregness Gdns	35 H6
Greig Ct	35 E1
Grosvenor Pl	34 C2
Grove Cres	32 B6
Guild St	35 F3

H

Street	Ref
Hamilton Pl	34 A2
Hammerfield Av	34 A5
Hammersmith Rd	34 B5
Hanover St	35 G1
Harcourt Rd	34 A1
Harlaw Pl	34 A4
Harlaw Rd	34 A4
Harlaw Ter	34 A4
Harriet St	35 E2
Harris Dr	32 D3
Harrow Rd	33 F3
Hartington Rd	34 B3
Hayfield Cres	32 B5
Hayfield Pl	32 B4
Hayton Rd	32 C3
Hermitage Av	33 E4
Highgate Gdns	35 F5
High St	33 E4
Hill St	34 D1
Hill Vw Gdns	35 G6
Hillview Rd	35 G6
Hilton Av	32 A4
Hilton Circle	32 B5
Hilton Ct	32 A4
Hilton Dr	32 B4
Hilton Pl	32 A4
Hilton Rd	32 A4
Hilton St	32 B5
Hilton Ter	32 B4
Hilton Wk	32 B4
Holburn Pl	34 D5
Holburn Rd	34 C4
Holburn St	34 D5
Holland Pl	32 D6
Holland St	32 D6
Hollybank Pl	34 D4
Hosefield Av	34 B1
Hosefield Rd	34 B1
Howburn Pl	34 D4
Hunter Pl	33 F6
Huntly St	34 D1
Hutcheon Ct	33 F1
Hutcheon Gdns	33 F1
Hutcheon St	34 D1
Hutchison Ter	34 A6

I

Street	Ref
Inverdon Ct	33 F2
Irvine Pl	34 D2

J

Street	Ref
Jacks Brae	34 D2
Jamaica St	32 D6
James St	35 G2

Name	Page	Ref
amiesons Quay	35	F3
asmine Pl	35	F1
asmine Ter	35	F1
asmine Way	35	F1
ohns Pk Pl	32	B1
ohn St	35	E1
opps La	35	E1
ubilee Gait	34	C6
ustice Mill La	34	D3
ute St	33	E6

K
Name	Page	Ref
Kerloch Gdns	35	F5
Kerloch Pl	35	F6
Kettocks Mill Rd	33	E2
Kidd St	34	D2
King George VI Br	35	E6
Kings Cres	33	F6
King's Gate	34	A2
Kingsland Pl	35	E1
King St	33	F5
King St (Woodside)	32	B3
Kinnaird Pl	32	D2
Kinord Circle	33	E1
Kintore Pl	34	D1
Kirkhill Pl	35	H6
Kirkhill Rd	35	G6
Kittybrewster Sq	32	C5

L
Name	Page	Ref
Laburnum Wk	32	A5
Ladywell Pl	35	H5
Lamond Pl	32	D6
Langstane Pl	35	E3
Laurel Av	32	B1
Laurel Braes	32	B1
Laurel Dr	32	A1
Laurel Gdns	32	B1
Laurel Gro	32	B1
Laurel Pl	32	A1
Laurel Rd	32	A1
Laurel Ter	32	B1
Laurel Vw	32	A1
Laurelwood Av	32	C5
Laurel Wynd	32	B1
Leadside Rd	34	D2
Learney Pl	34	A4
Lemon St	35	G1
Leslie Rd	32	C4
Leslie Ter	32	D5
Lilybank Pl	32	C4
Lime St	35	H2
Linksfield Ct	33	G4
Linksfield Gdns	33	F5
Linksfield Pl	33	F5
Linksfield Rd	33	F5
Links Pl	35	H2
Links Rd	35	H1
Links Rd (Bridge of Don)	33	G1
Links St	35	H2
Links Vw	33	G5
Livingstone Ct	33	F3
Loanhead Pl	34	C1
Loanhead Ter	34	C1
Loanhead Wk	34	C1
Loirston Pl	35	H5
Lord Hay's Ct	33	G2
Lord Hay's Gro	33	F2
Louisville Av	34	A4

M
Name	Page	Ref
Maberly St	35	E1
Mackie Pl	34	D2
Mansefield Pl	35	H5
Mansefield Rd	35	H4
Margaret Pl	34	C6
Marine Ter	35	E4
Market St	35	F2
Marischal St	35	F2
Marquis Rd	32	C3
Matthews Quay	35	H3
Mayfield Gdns	34	A4
Meadow La	32	D2
Meadow Pl	32	C2
Mearns Quay	35	H3
Mearns St	35	F2
Menzies Rd	35	G4
Merkland La	33	G5
Merkland Pl	33	F5
Merkland Rd	33	F5
Merkland Rd E	33	F5
Meston Wk	33	E4
Midchingle Rd	35	G3
Middlefield Cres	32	A3
Middlefield Ter	32	A3
Mile-End Av	34	B1
Mile-End La	34	B1
Mile-End Pl	34	B1
Millbank La	32	D6
Millbank Pl	32	D6
Millburn St	35	E4
Mill Ct	32	A2
Miller St	35	G2
Montgomery Cres	32	C2
Montgomery Rd	32	C2
Morgan Rd	32	A5
Morningfield Ms	34	A2
Morningside Gdns	34	A6
Morningside La	34	A6
Morningside Pl	34	A6
Morningside Rd	34	A6
Morningside Ter	34	A6
Morven Pl	35	G5
Mosman Gdns	32	A4
Mosman Pl	32	A4
Mounthooly	33	F6
Mounthooly Way	33	F6
Mount Pleasant	33	G1
Mount St	34	D1
Murray Ct	32	A2
Murray Ter	35	E5

N
Name	Page	Ref
Nellfield Pl	34	C4
Nelson Ct	33	F6
Nelson La	33	F6
Nelson St	33	F6
Newlands Av	34	B6
Newlands Cres	34	B6
Norfolk Rd	34	B5
North Esplanade E	35	G3
North Esplanade W	35	F4
Northfield Pl	34	D2
North Grampian Circle	35	G5
Northsea Ct	33	G3
Novar Pl	34	D1

O
Name	Page	Ref
Oakhill Cres	34	A2
Oakhill Rd	34	A2
Old Ch Rd	35	G6
Old Ford Rd	35	F4
Orchard Pl	33	E5
Orchard Rd	33	E5
Orchard St	33	E5
Orchard Wk	33	E5
Osborne Pl	34	B2
Oscar Pl	35	G5
Oscar Rd	35	G5

P
Name	Page	Ref
Palmerston Pl	35	F4
Palmerston Rd	35	F4
Park Rd	33	G6
Park St	35	G1
Pennan Rd	32	D2
Picktillum Av	32	C5
Picktillum Pl	32	C5
Pirie's Ct	32	C4
Pirie's La	32	C4
Pitstruan Pl	34	C4
Pitstruan Ter	34	C5
Pittodrie La	33	F5
Pittodrie Pl	33	F5
Pittodrie St	33	F5
Polmuir Av	35	E5
Polmuir Pl	35	E5
Polmuir Rd	35	E4
Polwarth Rd	35	F5
Portal Cres	32	D3
Portal Ter	32	D4
Portland St	35	E3
Powis Circle	32	D4
Powis Cres	32	D4
Powis La	33	E6
Powis Pl	32	D6
Powis Ter	32	D5
Poynernook Rd	35	F3
Primrosehill Dr	32	C4
Primrosehill Gdns	32	C4
Primrosehill Pl	32	C4
Prince Arthur St	34	C2
Princes St	35	F1
Printfield Ter	32	C3
Printfield Wk	32	C3
Promenade Ct	33	G4
Prospect Ct	35	F4
Prospect Ter	35	F4

Q
Name	Page	Ref
Queen Elizabeth II Br	35	F4
Queens Ct	34	A4
Queen's Cross	34	B3
Queens Gdns	34	B3
Queen's Gate	34	A3
Queens La N	34	B3
Queens La S	34	A3
Queens Links Leisure Pk	35	H1
Queens Ter	34	C3
Queen St	35	F2
Queen St (Woodside)	32	B3

R
Name	Page	Ref
Raeburn Pl	35	E1
Raeden Av	34	A1
Raeden Pk Rd	34	A1
Raik Rd	35	F3
Rattray Pl	32	D2
Regent Ct	33	G4
Regent Quay	35	G2
Regent Rd	35	G3
Regent Wk	33	G4
Richmondhill Ct	34	A2
Richmondhill Gdns	34	A1
Richmondhill Pl	34	A1
Richmondhill Rd	34	A1
Richmond St	34	D1
Richmond Ter	34	D1
Richmond Wk	34	D1
Ritchie Pl	32	C2
Riverside Dr	34	D6
Riverside Ter	34	C6
Rockall Pl	35	H5
Rockall Rd	35	H5
Rodger's Wk	35	E1
Rosebank Pl	34	D4
Rosebank Ter	35	E4
Rosebery St	34	B1
Rosehill Av	32	A4
Rosehill Ct	32	A5
Rosehill Cres	32	B4
Rosehill Dr	32	A4
Rosehill Pl	32	B4
Rosehill Ter	32	B4
Rosemount Pl	34	C1
Rosemount Viaduct	34	D2
Rose St	34	D2
Roslin Pl	35	G1
Roslin St	33	G6
Roslin Ter	33	F6
Rowan Rd	32	A5
Rubislaw Pl	34	D3
Rubislaw Ter	34	C3
Rubislaw Ter La	34	C3
Russell Rd	35	F4
Ruthrie Ct	34	B6
Ruthrieston Circle	34	C6
Ruthrieston Cres	34	C6
Ruthrieston Pl	34	C6
Ruthrieston Rd	34	B6

S
Name	Page	Ref
St. Andrew St	35	E1
St. Clair St	35	F1
St. Clement St	35	G2
St. Machar Dr	34	C2
St. Machar Ind Est	32	D3
St. Machar Pl	33	F3
St. Machar Rd	32	D3
St. Nicholas Cen	35	F2
St. Ninians Ct	33	F3
St. Ninians Pl	33	F2
St. Peter La	33	F6
St. Peter's Gate	33	F5
St. Peter's Pl	33	F5
St. Peter St	33	F6
St. Swithin Row	34	B3
St. Swithin St	34	B3
Salisbury Ct	34	C5
Salisbury Pl	34	C5
Salisbury Ter	34	B5
Sandilands Dr	32	C3
School Av	33	F4
School Dr	33	F4
Schoolhill	35	E2
School Rd	33	F4
School Ter	33	F4
School Wk	33	G4
Scotstown Gdns	33	F1
Seaforth Rd	33	F6
Seamount Rd	35	F1
Seaton Av	33	F3
Seaton Cres	33	G3
Seaton Dr	33	F3
Seaton Gdns	33	F3
Seaton Ho	33	G3
Seaton Pl	33	F3
Seaton Pl E	33	G3
Seaton Rd	33	F4
Seaton Wk	33	F3
Seaview Ho	33	G4
Seaview Rd	33	F1
Shiprow	35	F2
Short Loanings	34	C1
Simpson Rd	33	F1
Sinclair Pl	35	H4
Sinclair Rd	35	G4
Skene La	34	D2
Skene Sq	34	D1
Skene St	34	D2
Skene Ter	35	E2
Smithfield La	32	A3
Smithfield Rd	32	B3
Society La	32	B3
South Anderson Dr	34	B6
South Coll St	35	F3
South Crown St	35	E4
South Esplanade E	35	G4
South Esplanade W	35	F4
South Grampian Circle	35	G5
South Mile End	34	D3
South Mt St	34	D1
Spademill La	34	A3
Spademill Rd	34	A3
Spa St	35	E1
Spital	33	E5
Spital Wk	33	E5
Springbank St	35	E3
Springbank Ter	35	E3
Spring Gdn	35	E1
Stafford St	32	D6
Stanley St	34	C3
Station Rd	32	B2
Stell Rd	35	F3
Stewart Pk Ct	32	A4
Stewart Pk Pl	32	A4
Summerfield Ter	35	F1
Summer St	34	D2
Summer St (Woodside)	32	B3
Sunnybank Pl	33	E5
Sunnybank Rd	33	E5
Sunnyside Av	33	E5
Sunnyside Gdns	33	E5
Sunnyside Rd	32	D5
Sunnyside Ter	33	E5
Sycamore Pl	35	E5

T
Name	Page	Ref
Tanfield Av	32	C3
Tanfield Wk	32	C3
Tarbothill Rd	32	D1
Tedder Rd	32	D3
Tedder St	32	D3
Thistle Ct	34	D2
Thistle La	34	D2
Thistle Pl	34	D3
Thistle St	34	D3
Thomas Glover Pl	33	E1
Thomson St	34	C1
Thorngrove Av	34	A5
Thorngrove Ct	34	A5
Thorngrove Cres	34	A5
Thorngrove Pl	34	A5
Tillydrone Av	33	E3
Tillydrone Ct	33	D2
Tillydrone Rd	33	E3
Tillydrone Ter	32	D3
Trinity Quay	35	F2
Tullos Circle	35	G5
Tullos Cres	35	H5
Tullos Pl	35	H5

U
Name	Page	Ref
Union Glen	34	D3
Union Gro	34	C3
Union Gro La	34	C4
Union Row	34	D3
Union St	34	D3
Union Ter	35	E2
Union Wynd	34	D2
University Rd	33	E4
Upperkirkgate	35	F2
Urquhart La	33	F6
Urquhart Pl	33	G6
Urquhart Rd	33	F6
Urquhart St	33	G6
Urquhart Ter	33	G6

V
Name	Page	Ref
Victoria Br	35	G3
Victoria Rd	35	G4
Victoria St	34	D2
View Ter	34	D1
Virginia St	35	F2

W
Name	Page	Ref
Wales St	35	G1
Walker La	35	G4
Walker Pl	35	G4
Walker Rd	35	F5
Wallfield Cres	34	C2
Wallfield Pl	34	C2
Wapping St	35	F2
Waterloo Quay	35	G2
Watson La	34	C1
Watson St	34	C1
Wavell Cres	32	C2
Waverley La	34	D2
Waverley Pl	34	D3
Wellington Brae	35	F4
Wellington Br	35	F5
Wellington Pl	35	F5
Wellington Rd	35	F5
Wellington St	35	H2
Westburn Cres	32	B6
Westburn Dr	32	B5
Westburn Pk	32	C6
Westburn Rd	34	C1
Western Rd	32	C3
Westfield Rd	34	C2
Westfield Ter	34	C2
West Mt St	34	D1
West N St	35	F1
Whinhill Gdns	35	E5
Whinhill Gate	35	E5
Whinhill Rd	34	D5
Whitehall Pl	34	C2
Whitehall Rd	34	C2
Whitehall Ter	34	C2
Willowbank Rd	34	D4
Willowdale Pl	35	F1
Wingate Pl	32	D3
Wingate Rd	32	D3
Woolmanhill	35	E2

Y
Name	Page	Ref
York Pl	35	H2
York St	35	H2

This index contains streets that are not named on the map due to insufficient space. For each of these cases the nearest street that does appear on the map is shown in *italics*.

A
Abbotsford Pl 38 A5
Abbotsford St 38 A4
Adelaide Pl 38 C2
Adelaide Ter 38 C3
Airlie Pl 38 D5
Albany Ter 38 C3
Albert Sq
 off Commercial St 39 F4
Albert St 39 H2
Alexander St 39 E2
Alpin Rd 38 B1
Alpin Ter 38 B2
Alva Sq 39 E2
Anchor La 38 C4
Annfield Rd 38 B5
Annfield Row 38 B5
Annfield St 38 B5
Ann St 39 E3
Arbroath Rd 39 H2
Arklay St 39 F1
Arthurstone Ter 39 G2
Arthur St 39 E3
Artillery La 38 D5
Ashbank Rd 38 A4
Ash La
 off Ash St 38 C4
Ash St 38 C4

B
Baffin St 39 H2
Baffin Ter
 off Baffin St 39 H2
Baldovan Ter 39 H1
Balfield Rd 38 A1
Balfour St 38 D5
Balgayview Gdns 38 A2
Balmore St 39 G2
Baltic Gdns
 off Patons La 38 B6
Baltic La 39 E3
Bank Mill Rd 38 B4
Bank St 39 E4
Barrack Rd 38 D3
Barrack St 39 E4
Baxter Pk Ter 39 H1
Baxter St 38 B4
Bellefield Av 38 C6
Bellfield St 38 C5
Bell St 39 E4
Benvie Rd 38 B3
Birchwood Pl 38 A4
Blackness Av 38 A5
Blackness Rd 38 A4
Blackness St 38 B4
Blackness Ter 38 A5
Black St 38 B3
Blaikies Ms
 off Alexander St 39 E2
Blinshall St 38 D4
Blyth Pl 38 B4
Blyth St 38 B4
Bonnethill Ct
 off Hilltown Ter 39 E3
Bonnet Hill Pl 39 F3
Bonnybank Rd 39 F3
Brantwood Av 38 B1
Brantwood Pl
 off Brantwood Av 38 B1
Brewery La 38 C4
Brook St 38 C4
Brougham Gdns 39 G2
Broughty Ferry Rd 39 H3
Brown Constable St 39 G2
Brown St 38 D4
Bruce St 38 D1

Buchanan St 39 G2
Bucklemaker Ct
 off Harcourt St 38 D1
Burgess St 38 D1
Butterburn Ct
 off Strathmartine Rd 38 D1
Butterburn Sq 38 D1
Byron Cres 38 B1
Byron St 38 B1

C
Caldrum St 39 E2
Caldrum Ter 39 E2
Callender Gdns 39 G3
Campbell St 38 A2
Camperdown St 39 G4
Candle La 39 F4
Canning Pl 38 D1
Canning St 38 D1
Cardean St 39 H2
Carmichael Ct 38 D2
Carmichael Gdns 38 D2
Carmichael St 38 D2
Carnegie Sq
 off Ann St 39 E2
Carnegie St 39 E2
Carnegie Twr
 off Alexander St 39 F2
Castle St 39 F4
Catherine St 39 G1
Chapel St
 off Meadowside 39 E4
Church St 39 E2
City Quay Outlet Cen 39 G4
City Rd 38 A3
City Sq 39 F4
Clarendon Dr 38 A5
Clarendon Ter 38 A5
Cleghorn St 38 B3
Clepington St 39 F1
Cobden Pl 38 A2
Cobden St 38 A2
Colinton Pl 38 A3
Commercial St 39 F4
Constitution Rd 38 D3
Constitution St 38 D3
Constitution Ter 38 D3
Corso St 38 B5
Cotton Rd 39 F2
Coupar St 38 A2
Courthouse Sq 38 D4
Court St 39 G1
Coutties Wynd 39 E5
Cowan St 39 G2
Cowgate 39 F4
Craigie St 39 H2
Crescent La 39 G3
Crescent St 39 G3
Crichton St 39 F5
Cross La 38 D5
Cross Row 38 D5
Cunningham St 39 G2

D
Dalfield Ct
 off Hilltown Ter 39 E3
Daniel St 38 C4
Dens Brae 39 G3
Dens Rd 39 E1
Derby St 38 D1
Discovery Quay 39 E6
Dock St 39 F4
Dons Rd 39 E3
Douglas St 38 C4
Douglas Ter 38 C3

Drummond St 38 D2
Dudhope St 38 B3
Dudhope Cres Rd 39 E3
Dudhope St 39 E3
Dudhope Ter 38 C3
Dundonald St 39 F1
Dura St 39 G2
Dykehead Pl 39 G2

E
Eadies Rd 39 F3
Earl Grey Pl 39 F5
Eassons Angle 38 B4
East Dock St 39 G4
East Dock St
 Retail Pk 39 G3
East Hendersons
 Wynd 38 D4
East Marketgait 39 F3
East Somerville Pl 38 D3
Eastwell Rd 38 A1
East Whale La 39 G3
Edward St 38 C4
Eliza St 39 G1
Ellen St 39 F2
Elm St 38 A4
Erskine St 39 G2
Euclid Cres 39 E4
Euclid St 39 E4
Exchange St 39 F4

F
Fairbairn St 39 F1
Ferguson St 39 G3
Fingask St 38 D2
Fleuchar St 38 B4
Fords La
 off Perth Rd 38 B5
Forebank Rd 39 F3
Forebank St
 off Forebank Rd 39 F3
Forebank Ter
 off Forebank Rd 39 F3
Forester St 39 E4
Forest Pk Pl 38 B4
Forest Pk Rd 38 B4
Forfar Rd 39 H1
Fort St 38 A5
Forum Shop Cen 39 E4
Foundry La 39 G3
Fraser St 38 D1
Fullarton St 38 A2
Fyffe St 38 B4

G
Gardners La 38 C3
Gardner St 38 A2
Garland Pl 38 D3
Gellatly St 39 F4
Glamis St 39 E2
Glenagnes Rd 38 A4
Glenagnes St 38 A4
Glenesk Av 38 B1
Glenisla Ter 38 B1
Gordon Sq 38 A2
Gordon St 38 A2
Gowrie St 38 B5
Graham Pl 39 G3
Greenbank Pl 38 A3
Greenfield Pl 38 C5
Greenmarket 39 E5
Guthrie St 38 D4

H
Harcourt St 38 D1
Harlow Pl 38 B1
Harriet St 39 G1

Hastings Pl 38 D1
Hawkhill 38 C5
Hawkhill Pl 38 C5
High Mill Ct 38 B6
High St 39 E5
Hillbank Gdns 39 F2
Hillbank Pl
 off Hillbank Rd 39 F2
Hillbank Rd 39 F2
Hill Sq 39 E2
Hill St 38 D2
Hilltown 39 E2
Hilltown Ct
 off Hilltown Ter 39 E3
Hilltown Ter 39 E3
Horsewater Wynd 38 D4
Horse Wynd 39 F4
Hunter St 38 D4
Hyndford Pl 38 A5
Hyndford St 38 A4

I
Inverary Ter 38 B2
Inverlaw Pl 38 C3
Inverlaw Steps 38 C2
Isla St 39 E1

J
Jamaica Sq
 off Ann St 39 F2
Jamaica St 39 F2
Jamaica Twr
 off Alexander St 39 F2
James St 39 E2
Janefield Pl 39 H1
Johnston St 38 D4

K
Keats Pl 38 D1
Kemback St 39 H2
Kenmore Ter 38 B2
Kennet Wk 39 E2
Kilberry St 38 A2
Killin Av 38 B2
Kincaldrum Pl 39 E2
Kincardine St 38 C5
Kinghorne Ct
 off Kinghorne Rd 38 D2
Kinghorne Pl
 off Kinghorne Rd 38 D2
Kinghorne Rd 38 C2
Kinghorne Ter 38 B3
Kinghorne Wk 38 D2
King St 39 F3
King William St 39 F4
Kinloch St 38 D2
Kinloch Ter 38 D2
Kinnaird St 38 D2
Kinpurnie Pl 38 B1
Kirk La 39 F3

L
Laburn St
 off Constitution Rd 39 E3
Ladywell Av 39 F3
Laing Pl
 off Laing St 39 F2
Laing St 39 F2
Lambs La 39 F2
Langlands St 39 G2
Larch St 38 C4
Laurel Bk 39 F3
Law Cres 38 B1
Lawrence St 38 B4
Law Rd 38 C2
Lawside Av 38 B3
Lawside Rd 38 B2

awside Ter 38 B2
awson Pl 38 D2
aw St 38 C2
awton Rd 38 C1
awton Steps 38 C1
awton Ter 38 C1
eng St 38 D1
ilybank Rd 39 H3
ilybank Ter 39 H3
ime St 38 A4
ochee Rd 38 C3
oganlee Ter 38 A3
ogie Av 38 A4
ogie Gdns 38 A4
ogie St 38 A2
oons Rd 38 A2
orimer St 38 D1
ower Pleasance 38 C4
ower Princes St 39 G3
ynnewood Pl 39 H1
yon St 39 G2
ytton St 38 B5

M
lacaulay St 38 D2
lcDonald St 39 E3
lcGill St 39 H2
lcGonagall Sq
  off Patons La 38 B6
lcKinnon St 38 D2
lcVicars La 38 C5
lagdalen Pl 38 C6
lagdalen Yd Rd 38 B6
lains Rd 39 E1
lain St 39 E2
laitland St 39 G2
lalcolms Penn 38 D4
lalcolm St 39 G2
larine Par 39 G3
lartingale Gdns
  off Victoria Rd 39 G3
laryann La 39 F4
laryfield Ter 39 H1
lary Slessor Sq 39 G3
laxwelltown Twr
  off Alexander St 39 E2
leadow Entry
  off Commercial St 39 F4
leadow La 39 F4
leadow Pl Bldgs
  off Victoria Rd 39 E3
leadowside 39 E4
lelrose Ter 39 G1
lelville La 39 H3
lid Rd 39 E1
lid Wynd 38 C5
lillers Wynd 38 C5
lilnbank Rd 38 B4
lilnes E Wynd 38 C4
liln St 38 D4
lilton St 38 D1
linard Cres 38 C2
linto Pl 38 A5
litchell St 38 B3
lolison St 39 G1
lorgan Pl 39 H2
lorgan St 39 H1
lortimer St 38 D1
lurraygate 39 F4

N
eish St 39 F1
elson St 39 F2
elson Ter
  off Nelson St 39 F3
ethergate 38 D5
ew Inn Entry
  off High St 39 E4
icoll St 39 E4
orth Ellen St 39 F2

North Erskine St 39 G2
North George St 39 E2
North Isla St 39 F1
North Lindsay St 39 E4
North Marketgait 38 D4
North Somerville Pl 38 D2
North St 39 E1
North Wellington
  St 39 F2
North William St 39 F2

O
Ogilvie's Rd 39 E2
Ogilvie St 39 G2
Old Hawkhill 38 C5
Old Kings Cross Rd 38 A2
Osborne Pl 38 B6
Overgate Cen 39 E5

P
Palais Ct 39 E5
Panmure St 39 E4
Panmure Ter 38 D3
Paradise Rd 39 E3
Park Av 39 H2
Parker St 38 D3
Park Pl 38 D5
Park St 38 C4
Park Wynd 38 D5
Paterson St 38 D1
Patons La 38 B6
Patrick Pl 38 B6
Peddie St 38 A5
Peep O'day La 39 G3
Pennycook La 38 B5
Pentland Av 38 A3
Pentland Cres 38 A3
Perth Rd 38 C5
Peter St 39 F4
Pitfour St 38 A3
Pitkerro Rd 39 H1
Pleasance Ct
  off Douglas St 38 C4
Polepark Rd 38 B4
Pole St 38 B4
Powrie Pl 39 E3
Princes St 39 G3
Prospect Pl 39 E3

Q
Queen St 39 F3

R
Raglan St 39 H2
Rankine St 38 B3
Rattray St 39 E4
Reform St 39 E4
Reid Sq
  off Reid St 38 D1
Reid St 38 D2
Richmond Ter 38 A6
Ritchie's La
  off Hawkhill 38 B5
Riverside Dr 38 D6
Robertson St 39 H3
Rockwell Pl 38 C1
Roseangle 38 C6
Rosebank Pl 39 E3
Rosebank Rd 39 E3
Rosebank St 39 E2
Rosebery St 38 B3
Rosefield St 38 B4
Rosemount Ter
  *off Upper Constitution
  St* 38 D3
Royal Ex Ct
  off Commercial St 39 F4
Royal Ex La
  off Meadowside 39 E4

Russell Pl 38 D1
Ryehill La 38 B5

S
Saggar St 38 A3
St. Andrews La 39 F4
  off St. Andrews St
St. Andrews St 39 F4
St. Davids La
  off West Marketgait 38 D4
St. Mary Pl 38 B3
St. Mary St 38 C3
St. Matthews La 39 H3
St. Peter St 38 B5
St. Salvador St 39 E2
Salem St
  off Constitution Rd 39 E3
Scott St 38 A4
Seabraes 38 D6
Seabraes Ct 38 D6
Seabraes La 38 D5
Seafield Cl 38 C6
Seafield La 38 C6
Seafield Rd 38 C6
Seagate 39 F4
Session St 38 D4
Seymour Av 38 A5
Seymour St 38 A4
Shaftesbury Pk 38 A5
Shaftesbury Pl 38 A5
Shaftesbury Rd 38 A5
Shaftesbury Ter 38 A5
Shelley Gdns 38 D1
Shepherds Ln 38 B5
Shore Ter
  off Castle St 39 F4
Sibbald St 39 F1
Smalls La 38 D5
Smalls Wynd 38 D5
Soap Wks La 39 E3
Somerville Pl 38 D3
South Baffin St 39 H3
South George St 39 F3
South Marketgait 39 F5
South Tay St 38 D5
South Victoria
  Dock Rd 39 G4
South Ward Rd 39 E4
Speed St 38 A5
Spinners Wynd
  off Taylors La 38 B6
Springfield 38 C5
Stephen's Yd 38 B6
Step Row 38 B6
Stirling Av 38 D2
Stirling St 38 D2
Stirling Ter 38 D2
Stobswell Rd 39 G1
Strathmartine Rd 38 D1
Strathmore Av 38 B1
Strathmore St 39 F1
Strawberry Bk 38 B5
Sugarhouse Wynd 39 F3

T
Taits La 38 B5
Tannadice Ct 39 F1
  off Tannadice St
Tannadice St 39 E1
Tayfield Pl 38 B6
  off Patons La
Taylors La 38 B6
Tay Rd Br 39 G5
Tay Sq 39 E5
Tay St La 39 E5
Temple La 38 D5
Thistle St 39 E1
Thomson St 38 C6
Timber St 39 G4
Trades La 39 F4

Tullideph Pl 38 A2
Tullideph Rd 38 A2
Tullideph St 38 A3
Tulloch Ct
  off Hilltown Ter 39 E3

U
Union Pl 38 B5
Union St 39 E5
Union Ter 38 D3
Upper Constitution
  St 38 D2
Ure St 38 C5
Urquhart St 38 C4

V
Victoria Rd 39 E3
Victoria St 39 G3

W
Walker's Mill 39 F1
Walton St 38 C4
Ward Rd 38 D4
Watsons La
  off Hawkhill 38 C4
Watson St 39 H3
Weavers Yd 39 G3
Wellbank La 38 A1
Wellgate Cen 39 F3
Wellington Sq
  off Ann St 39 F3
Wellington St 39 F2
Wellington Twr
  off Alexander St 39 F2
Well Rd 38 C5
West Bell St 38 D4
Westfield Av 38 C5
Westfield La 38 C6
Westfield Pl 38 C6
West Hendersons
  Wynd 38 D4
West Lyon St 39 G2
West Marketgait 38 D4
West Port 38 D5
West Somerville Pl 38 D3
West St 38 D1
West Victoria
  Dock Rd 39 G4
West Wf Rd 39 G4
West Wynd 38 C5
Wetherby Pl 38 C1
Whistler's Way
  off Ann St 39 E3
Whitehall Cres 39 E5
Whitehall St 39 E5
Wilkies La 38 C4
William Barclay Sq 39 E3
William St 39 F2
Willison St 39 E4
Windsor Pl
  off Magdalen Yd Rd 38 B6
Windsor St 38 A5
Windsor Ter 38 A5
Wishart St
  off Stirling Ter 38 D2
Wolseley St 39 G1

Y
Yeaman Shore
  off Union St 39 E5

DUNDEE

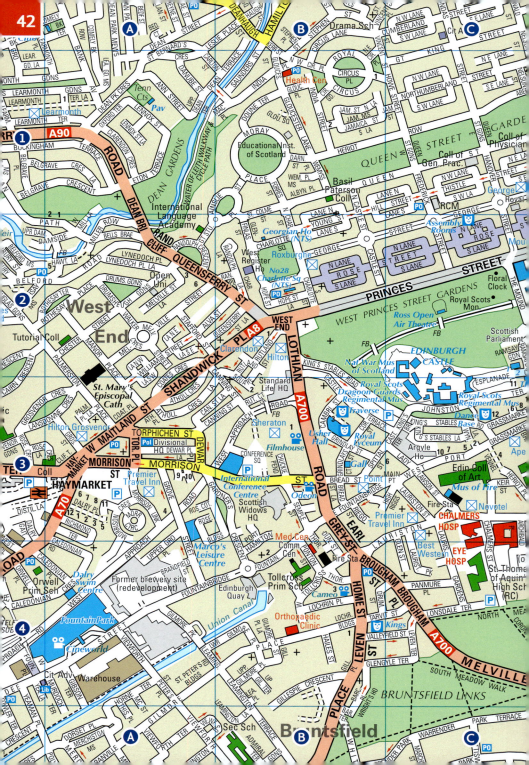

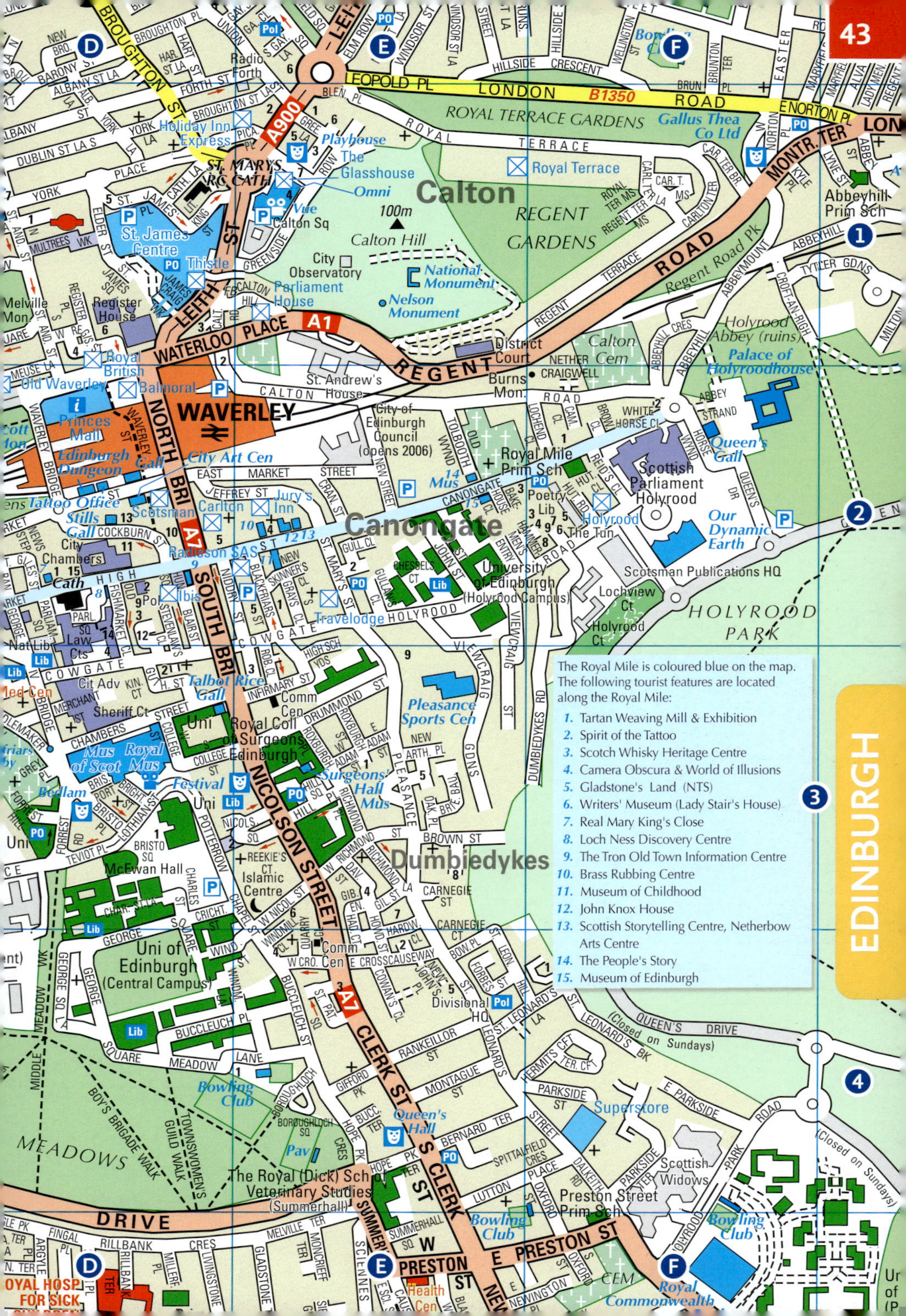

EDINBURGH

The Royal Mile is coloured blue on the map. The following tourist features are located along the Royal Mile:

1. Tartan Weaving Mill & Exhibition
2. Spirit of the Tattoo
3. Scotch Whisky Heritage Centre
4. Camera Obscura & World of Illusions
5. Gladstone's Land (NTS)
6. Writers' Museum (Lady Stair's House)
7. Real Mary King's Close
8. Loch Ness Discovery Centre
9. The Tron Old Town Information Centre
10. Brass Rubbing Centre
11. Museum of Childhood
12. John Knox House
13. Scottish Storytelling Centre, Netherbow Arts Centre
14. The People's Story
15. Museum of Edinburgh

Calton

Calton Hill

REGENT GARDENS

ROYAL TERRACE GARDENS

LONDON ROAD B1350

Gallus Thea Co Ltd

Royal Terrace

National Monument

Nelson Monument

City Observatory

Parliament House

Holyrood Abbey (ruins)

Palace of Holyroodhouse

Queen's Gall

Scottish Parliament Holyrood

Our Dynamic Earth

Scotsman Publications HQ

HOLYROOD PARK

Regent Road Pk

WAVERLEY

St. Andrew's House

District Court

Burns Mon.

Craigwell

Royal Mile Prim Sch

Poetry Lib

Holyrood

The Tun

Canongate

City Art Cen

Jury's Inn

Scotsman

Carlton

Robertson SAS

City Chambers

Cath

Law

Nat Lib

Talbot Rice Gall

Comm Cen

Royal Coll of Surgeons Edinburgh

Pleasance Sports Cen

Surgeons' Hall Mus

University of Edinburgh (Holyrood Campus)

Travelodge HOLYROOD

Dumbiedykes

Lochview Ct

Holyrood Ct

Superstore

Scottish Widows

Mus of Scot Mus

Festival

Bedlam

Uni

McEwan Hall

REEKIE'S CT

Islamic Centre

Uni of Edinburgh (Central Campus)

Divisional Pol

Bowling Club

Queen's Hall

The Royal (Dick) School Veterinary Studies (Summerhall)

Preston Street Prim Sch

Bowling Club

Royal Commonwealth

MEADOWS

DRIVE

ROYAL HOSP FOR SICK

St James Centre

St. Mary's RC Cath

Playhouse

The Glasshouse

Omni

Vue

Calton Sq

Thistle

Holiday Inn Express

Radio Forth

Register House

Melville Mon

Old Waverley

Royal British

Balmoral

Princes Mall

Edinburgh Dungeon

Tattoo Office

Stills Gall

Ibis

Abbeyhill Prim Sch

1

2

3

4

D
E
F

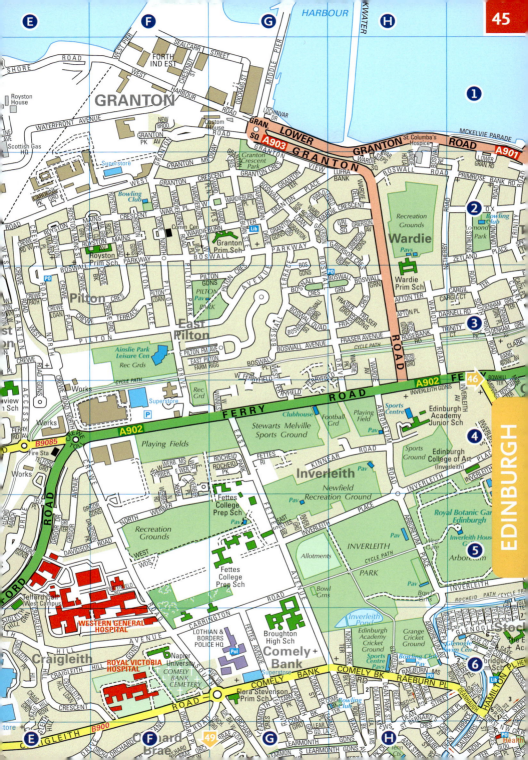

EDINBURGH

Index to streets

There are street names in this index which are followed by a number in **bold**. These numbers can be found on the map where there is insufficient space to show the street name in full.

A

Abbeyhill 43 F2
Abbeyhill Cres 43 F2
Abbeyhill Ind Est 51 F1
Abbey La 51 F1
Abbeymount 43 F1
Abbey Strand 43 F2
Abbey St 51 F1
Abbotsford Ct 49 H6
Abbotsford Cres 49 H6
Abbotsford Pk 49 H6
Abercorn Cres 51 H2
Abercorn Dr 51 H2
Abercorn Gro 51 H2
Abercorn Rd 51 H2
Abercromby Pl 42 C1
Abinger Gdns 49 E3
Academy Pk 47 F4
Academy St 47 F4
Admiral Ter 50 A5
Admiralty St 47 E2
Advocates Cl 1 43 D2
Afton Pl 45 H3
Afton Ter 45 H3
Agnew Ter 46 C3
Ainslie Pl 42 A1
Aird's Cl 42 C3
Aitkenhill 48 C6
Albany La 43 D1
Albany St 43 D1
Albany St La 43 D1
Albert Dock 47 F2
Albert Pl 46 D6
Albert Rd 47 G3
Albert St 47 E5
Albert Ter 49 H6
Albion Business
Cen 47 F6
Albion Gdns 47 F6
Albion Pl 47 F6
Albion Rd 47 F6
Albion Ter 47 F6
Albyn Pl 42 B1
Alderbank Pl 49 F6
Alderbank Ter 49 F6
Alemoor Cres 47 G5
Alemoor Pk 47 G5
Alexander Dr 49 E5
Alfred Pl 51 E5
Allanfield 47 E6
Allanfield Pl 47 E6
Allan St 45 H6
Almondbank Ter 49 F6
Alvanley Ter 1 50 A5
Alva Pl 51 F1
Alva St 42 A2
Anchor Cl 11 43 D2
Anchorfield 46 C2
Anderson Pl 46 D3
Andrew Wd Ct 46 B2
Angle Pk Ter 49 G5
Annandale St 46 C5
Annandale St La 46 D6
Annfield 46 C2
Annfield St 46 C2
Ann St 42 A1
Ann Ter 51 F1
Antigua St 1 46 D6
Appin Ter 49 E6
Arboretum Av 45 H6
Arboretum Pl 45 H5
Arboretum Rd 45 H4
Archibald Pl 42 C3
Arden St 50 B5
Ardmillan Pl 49 G5
Ardmillan Ter 49 F5
Ardmillan Ter La 1 49 G5
Argyle Pk Ter 50 C5
Argyle Pl 50 C5
Argyle St 46 D2
Argyll Ter 2 42 A3
Arthur St 47 E5

Arthur St La 47 E5
Ashley Gro 49 F6
Ashley Pl 46 D4
Ashley Ter 49 F6
Ashville Ter 47 G5
Assembly St 47 F3
Atholl Cres 42 A3
Atholl Cres La 42 A3
Atholl Pl 42 A3
Atholl Ter 3 42 A3
Auchinleck Ct 46 C2
Auchinleck's
Brae 1 46 B2
Avenue Vil 45 G6
Avondale Pl 46 A6

B

Back Dean 49 G2
Baird Av 48 D4
Baird Dr 48 C5
Baird Gdns 48 D4
Baird Gro 48 D4
Baird Ter 48 D4
Bakehouse Cl 43 E2
Baker's Pl 1 46 A6
Balbirnie Pl 49 F3
Balfour Pl 46 D5
Balfour St 47 E4
Balgreen Av 48 B4
Balgreen Gdns 48 B4
Balgreen Pk 48 B4
Balgreen Rd 48 B4
Ballantyne La 1 47 E3
Ballantyne Rd 47 E3
Balmoral Pl 46 A6
Baltic St 47 F3
Bangholm Av 46 A3
Bangholm
Bower Av 46 A3
Bangholm Gro 46 B3
Bangholm Ln 46 B3
Bangholm Pk 46 A3
Bangholm Pl 46 A3
Bangholm Rd 46 A3
Bangholm Ter 46 A4
Bangholm Vw 46 B3
Bangor Rd 46 D3
Bank St 43 D2
Barclay Pl 42 B4
Barclay Ter 50 A5
Baronscourt Rd 51 H1
Barony Pl 3 46 C6
Barony St 46 C6
Barrie's Cl 14 43 D2
Bathfield 46 D2
Bath Rd 47 G3
Baxter's Pl 1 43 E1
Beaufort Rd 50 C6
Beaverbank
Business Pk 46 B5
Beaverbank Pl 46 C5
Beaverhall Rd 46 C5
Bedford Ct 45 H6
Bedford St 45 H6
Beechmount Cres 48 C3
Beechmount Pk 48 C4
Beechwood Mains 48 C3
Beechwood Ter 47 G5
Belford Av 49 F1
Belford Br 49 G2
Belford Gdns 49 F1
Belford Ms 49 G2
Belford Pk 49 G2
Belford Pl 49 F2
Belford Rd 49 G2
Belford Ter 1 49 G2
Belgrave Cres 49 G1
Belgrave Cres La 49 G1
Belgrave Ms 49 G1
Belgrave Pl 49 G1
Bellevue 46 C6
Bellevue Cres 46 C6
Bellevue Gdns 46 C5

Bellevue Gro 46 C6
Bellevue La 46 C6
Bellevue Pl 46 C6
Bellevue Rd 46 C6
Bellevue St 46 C6
Bellevue Ter 46 C5
Bell Pl 46 A6
Bells Brae 42 A2
Bell's Mills 49 G2
Bell's Wynd 2 43 D2
Belmont Av 48 C3
Belmont Cres 48 C3
Belmont Dr 48 C3
Belmont Gdns 48 C3
Belmont Pk 48 C3
Belmont Ter 48 C3
Belmont Vw 48 C3
Belvedere Pk 46 B2
Beresford Av 46 B2
Beresford Gdns 46 B3
Beresford Pl 46 A3
Beresford Ter 46 A3
Bernard St 47 F2
Bernard Ter 43 E4
Bethlehem Way 47 G5
Birnies Ct 44 B3
Blackadder Pl 45 F2
Blacket Av 51 E5
Blacket Pl 51 E5
Blackford Rd 50 B6
Blackfriars St 43 E2
Blackie Rd 47 F6
Blackwood Cres 50 D5
Blair St 43 D2
Blandfield 46 C5
Blantyre Ter 49 H6
Bleachfield 46 C4
Blenheim Pl 43 E1
Blinkbonny Av 46 A3
Blinkbonny Cres 48 D1
Blinkbonny Gdns 49 E1
Blinkbonny Gro 49 E1
Blinkbonny Gro W 49 E1
Blinkbonny Rd 49 E1
Blinkbonny Ter 48 D1
Boat Grn 46 B5
Bonar Pl 46 C3
Bonnington Av 46 C3
Bonnington
Gait 1 46 D4
Bonnington Gro 46 C3
Bonnington
Ind Est 46 D4
Bonnington Rd 46 D4
Bonnington Rd La 46 D4
Bonnington Ter 46 C3
Bonnyhaugh 46 C4
Bonnyhaugh La 46 C4
Boothacre Cotts 2 47 H4
Boothacre La 47 H4
Boroughloch 43 E4
Boroughloch Sq 43 E4
Borthwick Pl 49 F3
Borthwick's Cl 3 43 D2
Boswall Av 45 G3
Boswall Cres 45 G3
Boswall Dr 45 G2
Boswall Gdns 45 G3
Boswall Grn 45 H3
Boswall Gro 45 G3
Boswall Ln 45 G2
Boswall Ms 45 G2
Boswall Parkway 45 F2
Boswall Pl 45 G3
Boswall Quad 45 G3
Boswall Rd 45 H2
Boswall Sq 45 G3
Boswall Ter 45 G3
Bothwell St 47 E6
Bowhill Ter 46 A4
Bowie's Cl 1 47 F3
Bowling Grn, The 47 E3
Bowling La 8 47 E3

Bowmont Pl 43 E4
Boyd's Entry 2 43 E2
Boy's Brigade Wk 43 D4
Brandfield St 42 A4
Brandon St 46 B6
Brandon Ter 46 B6
Breadalbane St 46 D3
Breadalbane Ter 5 42 A3
Bread St 42 B3
Bread St La 42 B3
Brewery La 1 47 E3
Briarbank Ter 49 F6
Bridge Pl 45 H6
Briery Bauks 43 E3
Brighton St 43 D3
Bright's Cres 51 E6
Bright Ter 8 42 A3
Bristo Pl 43 D3
Bristo Port 43 D3
Bristo Sq 43 D3
Broad Wynd 7 47 F3
Broomhouse Row 48 A6
Brougham Pl 42 C4
Brougham St 42 B4
Broughton Mkt 46 C6
Broughton Pl 46 C6
Broughton Pl La 46 C6
Broughton Rd 46 C5
Broughton St 46 C6
Broughton St La 43 D1
Brown's Cl 43 F2
Brown's Pl 4 42 C3
Brown St 42 E3
Brown St La 8 43 E3
Brunswick Pl 46 D6
Brunswick Rd 46 D6
Brunswick St 46 D6
Brunswick St La 46 D6
Brunswick Ter 1 47 E6
Brunton Gdns 2 47 E6
Brunton Pl 47 E6
Brunton Ter 47 E6
Bruntsfield Av 50 A5
Bruntsfield Cres 50 A5
Bruntsfield Gdns 50 A6
Bruntsfield Pl 49 H6
Bruntsfield Ter 50 A5
Bryson Rd 49 G5
Buccleuch Pl 43 D4
Buccleuch St 43 E4
Buccleuch Ter 43 E4
Buchanan St 47 E5
Buckingham Ter 49 G1
Bull's Cl 5 43 F2
Burgess St 47 F3
Burgess Ter 51 F6
Burlington St 47 E3
Burns St 47 F4

C

Cables Wynd 47 E3
Cables Wynd Ho 47 E3
Cadiz St 47 F3
Cadzow Pl 51 F1
Caithness Pl 46 A3
Caledonian Cres 49 G4
Caledonian Pl 42 A4
Caledonian Rd 42 A4
Calton Hill 43 E1
Calton Rd 43 E2
Calton Sq 43 E1
Cambridge Av 46 D5
Cambridge Gdns 46 D5
Cambridge St 42 B3
Cambridge St La 3 42 B3
Cambusnethan St 51 G1
Cameron Ho Av 51 G6
Campbell Av 48 D3
Campbell Rd 48 D2
Campbell's Cl 43 F2
Candlemaker Row 43 D3
Canning St 42 A2
Canning St La 42 A3

Cannon Wynd 46 D2
Canon Ct 3 46 B5
Canongate 43 E2
Canon La 46 B6
Canonmills 46 B5
Canonmills Br 2 46 B5
Canon St 46 B6
Carberry Pl 49 F3
Carfrae Gdns 44 B6
Carfrae Gro 44 B6
Carfrae Pk 44 B6
Carfrae Rd 44 B6
Cargil Ct 45 H3
Cargil Ter 46 A3
Carlton St 42 A1
Carlton Ter 43 F1
Carlton Ter Brae 43 F1
Carlton Ter La 43 F1
Carlton Ter Ms 43 F1
Carlyle Pl 51 F1
Carnegie Ct 43 E3
Carnegie St 43 E3
Caroline Pk Av 45 E1
Caroline Pk Gro 45 E2
Carpet La 47 F3
Carrick Knowe Av 48 A4
Carrick Knowe
Gdns 48 A5
Carrick Knowe Gro 48 A5
Carrick Knowe
Hill 48 A5
Carrick Knowe Pl 48 A5
Carrick Knowe Ter 48 A5
Carrington Rd 45 F6
Carron Pl 47 G3
Carrubber's Cl 5 43 D2
Casselbank St 47 E4
Cassel's La 47 E4
Castlehill 42 C2
Castle St 42 B2
Castle Ter 42 B3
Castle Wynd N 11 42 C3
Castle Wynd S 6 42 C3
Cathcart Pl 49 G4
Cathedral La 43 D1
Catherine Pl 46 B5
Causeway, The 51 H4
Causewayside 50 D5
Chalmers Bldgs 2 42 B4
Chalmers Cl 4 43 E2
Chalmers Cres 50 C5
Chalmers St 42 C3
Chamberlain Rd 50 A6
Chambers St 43 D3
Chancelot Cres 46 B3
Chancelot Gro 46 B3
Chancelot Ter 46 C3
Chapel La 2 47 F3
Chapel St 43 D3
Chapel Wynd 7 42 C3
Charlesfield 1 43 D3
Charles St 43 D3
Charles St La 43 D3
Charlotte La 42 B2
Charlotte Sq 42 B2
Chessels Ct 43 E2
Chesser Av 48 C6
Chesser Cotts 1 48 D6
Chesser Ct 48 C6
Chesser Gdns 48 C6
Chester St 42 A2
Chestnut St 45 F1
Cheyne St 45 H6
Chuckie Pend 42 B3
Church Hill 50 A6
Church Hill Dr 50 A6
Church Hill Pl 50 A6
Circus Gdns 42 B1
Circus La 46 A6
Circus Pl 42 B1
Citadel Ct 47 E2
Citadel Pl 47 E2
Citadel St 2 47 E2

Clarebank Cres	47 G4
Claremont Bk	46 C6
Claremont Ct	46 C5
Claremont Cres	46 C5
Claremont Gdns	47 G4
Claremont Gro	46 C5
Claremont Pk	47 G4
Claremont Rd	47 G4
Clarence St	46 A6
Clarendon Cres	42 A1
Clark Av	46 B3
Clark Pl	46 A3
Clark Rd	46 A3
Clearburn Cres	51 G6
Clearburn Gdns	51 G6
Clearburn Rd	51 G6
Clerk St	43 E4
Clifton Ter	42 A3
Clinton Rd	50 A6
Clockmill La	51 G1
Coalhill	47 E3
Coates Cres	42 A3
Coates Gdns	49 G3
Coates Pl	42 A3
Coatfield La	47 F3
Cobden Cres	51 E6
Cobden Rd	51 E6
Cobden Ter 7	42 A3
Coburg St	47 E3
Cochrane Pl 1	47 F4
Cochran Pl	46 C6
Cochran Ter	46 C6
Cockburn St	43 D2
Coffin La	49 G4
Coinyie Ho Cl 1	43 E2
College Wynd 2	43 D3
Collins Pl	46 A6
Coltbridge Av	49 E3
Coltbridge Gdns	49 F3
Coltbridge Millside	49 F3
Coltbridge Ter	49 E3
Coltbridge Vale	49 F3
Columba Av	44 C6
Columba Rd	44 C6
Colville Pl	46 A6
Comely Bk	45 G6
Comely Bk Av	45 H6
Comely Bk Gro	49 G1
Comely Bk Pl	45 H6
Comely Bk Pl Ms 2	45 H6
Comely Bk Rd	45 H6
Comely Bk Row	45 H6
Comely Bk St	45 G6
Comely Bk Ter	45 G6
Comely Grn Cres	51 F1
Comely Grn Pl	51 F1
Commercial St	47 E2
Commercial Wf 1	47 F2
Conference Sq	42 B3
Connaught Pl	46 C3
Considine Gdns	51 H1
Considine Ter	51 H1
Constitution St	47 E4
Convening Ct 1	42 A2
Cooper's Cl 3	43 F2
Corbiehill Av	44 B5
Corbiehill Cres	44 A5
Corbiehill Gdns	44 B5
Corbiehill Gro	44 B5
Corbiehill Pk	44 A5
Corbiehill Pl	44 A5
Corbiehill Rd	44 A5
Corbiehill Ter	44 A5
Cornhill Ter	47 G4
Cornwallis Pl	46 B6
Cornwall St	42 B3
Coronation Wk	42 C4
Corstorphine Rd	48 D3
Corunna Pl	47 E3
Cottage Pk	48 B1
Couper Fld	47 E2
Couper St	47 E2
Cowan Rd	49 F6
Cowan's Cl	43 E4
Cowgate	43 D3
Cowgatehead	43 D3
Coxfield	48 D6
Coxfield La 2	48 D6
Craigcrook Av	44 B6
Craigcrook Gdns	48 C1
Craigcrook Gro	48 B1
Craigcrook Pk	48 B1
Craigcrook Pl 1	44 D6
Craigcrook Rd	48 C1
Craigcrook Sq	44 C6
Craigcrook Ter	44 C6
Craighall Av	46 B2
Craighall Bk	46 B2
Craighall Cres	46 B2
Craighall Gdns	46 B3
Craighall Rd	46 B2
Craighall Ter	46 B3
Craigleith Av N	48 D2
Craigleith Av S	48 D2
Craigleith Cres	48 D1
Craigleith Dr	48 D1
Craigleith Gdns	48 D1
Craigleith Gro	48 D1
Craigleith Hill	49 E1
Craigleith Hill Av	44 D6
Craigleith Hill Cres	45 E6
Craigleith Hill Gdns	45 E6
Craigleith Hill Grn	45 E6
Craigleith Hill Gro	45 E6
Craigleith Hill Ln	45 E6
Craigleith Hill Pk	45 E6
Craigleith Hill Row	45 E6
Craigleith Retail Pk	45 E6
Craigleith Ri	48 D2
Craigleith Rd	49 E1
Craigleith Vw	48 D2
Craigmuir Pl	44 D3
Craigroyston Gro	44 B4
Craigroyston Pl	44 B3
Cranston St	43 E2
Crarae Av	49 E2
Crawford Br 1	47 F6
Crewe Bk	45 F3
Crewe Cres	45 F3
Crewe Gro	45 F3
Crewe Ln	45 E3
Crewe Path	45 E3
Crewe Pl	45 E3
Crewe Rd Gdns	45 E3
Crewe Rd N	45 E3
Crewe Rd S	45 E4
Crewe Rd W	45 E3
Crewe Ter	45 E3
Crewe Toll	45 E4
Crichton's Cl 4	43 F2
Crichton St	43 D3
Crighton Pl	47 E5
Croall Pl	46 D6
Croft-an-righ	43 F1
Cromwell Pl	47 E2
Crown Pl	43 F2
Crown St	47 E4
Cumberland St	46 B6
Cumberland St N E La	46 B6
Cumberland St N W La	46 B6
Cumberland St S E La	46 B6
Cumberland St S W La	46 B6
Cumin Pl	50 D5
Cumlodden Av	48 D2
Cunningham Pl 1	47 E4

D

Daisy Ter 3	49 F6
Dalgety Av	47 G6
Dalgety Rd	47 G6
Dalgety St	51 G1
Dalkeith Rd	43 F4
Dalmeny Rd	46 C3
Dalmeny St	47 E5
Dalry Gait	49 G3
Dalrymple Cres	50 D6
Dalry Pl	42 A3
Dalry Rd	49 G4
Dalziel Pl 1	51 F1
Damside	49 G2
Dania Ct	48 A6
Danube St	42 A1
Darnaway St	42 B1
Darnell Rd	45 H3
Davidson Gdns	44 B5
Davidson Pk	45 E5
Davidson Rd	45 E5
Davie St	43 E3
Dean Bk La	46 A6
Dean Br	42 A1
Deanery Cl 1	51 H1
Deanhaugh St	46 A6
Dean Pk Cres	42 A1
Dean Pk Ms	45 H6
Dean Pk St	45 H6
Dean Path	49 G1
Dean Path Bldgs 2	42 A2
Dean St	45 H6
Dean Ter	42 A1
Delhaig	48 D6
Denham Grn Av	46 A3
Denham Grn Pl	46 A3
Denham Grn Ter	46 A3
Derby St	46 C2
Devon Pl	49 G3
Dewar Pl	42 A3
Dewar Pl La	42 A3
Dick Pl	50 C6
Dicksonfield	46 D6
Dickson's Cl 5	43 E2
Dickson St	47 E5
Distillery La	49 G3
Dock Pl	47 E2
Dock St	47 E2
Dorset Pl	49 H5
Douglas Cres	49 G2
Douglas Gdns	49 G2
Douglas Gdns Ms 3	49 G2
Douglas Ter 1	42 A3
Doune Ter	42 B1
Downfield Pl	49 G4
Downie Gro	48 A4
Downie Ter	48 A4
Drumdryan St	42 B3
Drummond Pl	46 B6
Drummond St	43 E3
Drumsheugh Gdns	42 A2
Drumsheugh Pl 3	42 A2
Drum Ter	47 F6
Dryden Gait	46 D5
Dryden Gdns	46 D5
Dryden Pl	51 E5
Dryden St	46 D5
Dryden Ter	46 D5
Drylaw Av	44 D6
Drylaw Cres	44 C6
Drylaw Gdns	44 C5
Drylaw Grn	44 C6
Drylaw Gro	44 C6
Drylaw Ho Gdns	44 C5
Drylaw Ho Paddock	44 C5
Dublin Meuse	43 D1
Dublin St	46 C6
Dublin St La N	46 C6
Dublin St La S	43 D1
Dudley Av	46 C2
Dudley Av S	46 D3
Dudley Bk	46 C2
Dudley Cres	46 C2
Dudley Gdns	46 C2
Dudley Gro	46 C2
Dudley Ter	46 C2
Duff Rd	49 G4
Duff St	49 G4
Duff St La	49 G4
Duke Pl	47 F4
Duke St	47 F4
Duke St Glebe	47 F4
Duke's Wk	51 G2
Dumbiedykes Rd	43 F3
Dunbar St	42 B3
Duncan Pl	47 F4
Duncan St	50 D6
Dundas St	46 B6
Dundee St	49 G4
Dundee Ter	49 G5
Dundonald St	46 B6
Dunedin St	46 C5
Dunlop's Ct 12	42 C3
Dunrobin Pl	46 A6

E

Earl Grey St	42 B3
Earl Haig Gdns	46 A3
Earl Haig Homes	48 B6
Earlston Pl	51 F1
East Adam St	43 E3
East Broughton Pl 1	46 C6
East Castle Rd	49 H5
East Claremont St	46 C6
East Ct 2	48 D1
East Cromwell St	47 E2
East Crosscauseway	43 E4
Easter Belmont Rd	48 C3
Easter Dalry Dr	49 G4
Easter Dalry Pl 1	49 G3
Easter Dalry Rigg 3	49 G4
Easter Dalry Rd	49 G3
Easter Dalry Wynd	49 G3
Easter Drylaw Av	44 D5
Easter Drylaw Bk	44 D4
Easter Drylaw Dr	45 E5
Easter Drylaw Gdns	44 D5
Easter Drylaw Gro	44 D5
Easter Drylaw Ln	44 D4
Easter Drylaw Pl	44 D4
Easter Drylaw Vw	44 D4
Easter Drylaw Way	44 D5
Easter Hermitage	47 G5
Easter Rd	47 E6
Easter Warriston	46 B4
East Fettes Av	45 G5
East Fountainbridge	42 B3
East Hermitage Pl	47 F4
East Lillypot	46 A3
East London St	46 C6
East Mkt St	43 D2
East Mayfield	51 E6
East Montgomery Pl	47 E6
East Newington Pl	50 D5
East Norton Pl	43 F1
East Parkside	43 F4
East Pilton Fm Av	45 F3
East Pilton Fm Rigg	45 F3
East Preston St	50 D5
East Preston St La 3	43 E4
East Restalrig Ter	47 G4
East Sciennes St	50 D5
East Scotland St La	46 C6
East Silvermills La	46 A6
East Trinity Rd	46 A3
East Werberside	45 F4
East Werberside Pl	45 F4
Edina Pl	47 E6
Edina St	47 E6
Edinburgh Dock	47 G2
Eglinton Cres	49 G3
Eglinton St 3	49 F3
Eildon St	46 B5
Eildon Ter	46 A5
Elbe St	47 F3
Elder St	43 D1
Elder St E 5	43 D1
Elgin Pl	49 G3
Elgin St	47 E6
Elgin St N	47 E6
Elgin Ter	47 E6
Elizafield	46 D4
Ellersly Rd	48 C3
Elliot St	47 E6
Elm Pl 2	47 G4
Elm Row	46 D6
Elmwood Ter	47 G4
Eltringham Gdns	48 D6
Eltringham Gro	48 D6
Eltringham Ter	48 D6
Esdaile Bk	50 C6
Esdaile Gdns	50 C6
Esdaile Pk 1	50 C6
Esplanade	42 C3
Eton Ter	42 A1
Ettrickdale Pl	46 A5
Ettrick Gro	49 H5
Ettrick Ln	49 G6
Ettrick Rd	49 G6
Eyre Cres	46 B6
Eyre Pl	46 B6
Eyre Pl La	46 B6
Eyre Ter	46 B6

F

Falcon Gdns	50 A6
Ferryfield	45 G4
Ferry Gait Cres	44 B4
Ferry Gait Dr	44 B4
Ferry Gait Gdns	44 B4
Ferry Gait Pl	44 B4
Ferry Gait Wk	44 B4
Ferrylee	46 D2
Ferry Rd	46 C3
Ferry Rd Av	45 E4
Ferry Rd Dr	45 E3
Ferry Rd Gdns	44 D4
Ferry Rd Gro	44 D4
Ferry Rd Pl	44 D4
Festival Sq 1	42 B3
Fettes Av	45 G6
Fettes Ri	45 G4
Fettes Row	46 B6
Fidra Ct	44 B3
Findhorn Pl	50 D5
Findlay Av	47 H5
Findlay Cotts	47 H5
Findlay Gdns	47 H5
Findlay Gro	47 H5
Findlay Medway	47 H5
Fingal Pl	50 C5
Fingzies Pl 3	47 G4
Fishmarket Sq 2	46 C1
Fleshmarket Cl 13	43 D2
Forbes Rd	50 A6
Forbes St	43 E4
Ford's Rd	48 C6
Forres St	42 B1
Forrest Hill	43 D3
Forrest Rd	43 D3
Forth Ind Est	45 F1
Fort Ho	46 D2
Forth St	43 D1
Forthview Rd	44 D6
Forthview Ter	44 C6
Fountainbridge	42 B4
Fowler Ter	49 G5
Fox St	47 G3
Fraser Av	45 H3
Fraser Cres	45 H3
Fraser Gdns	45 H3
Fraser Gro	45 H3
Frederick St	42 C1

G

Gabriel's Rd 6	43 D1
Gabriel's Rd (Stockbridge) 6	46 A6

EDINBURGH

Name	Ref
Gardiner Gro	44 C6
Gardiner Rd	44 C6
Gardiner Ter	48 C1
Gardner's Cres	42 A3
Garscube Ter	49 E2
Gayfield Cl	46 D6
Gayfield Pl	46 D6
Gayfield Pl La	46 D6
Gayfield Sq	46 D6
Gayfield St	46 C6
Gayfield St La	46 C6
Gentle's Entry 8	43 F2
George IV Br	43 D2
George Sq	43 D4
George Sq La	43 D4
George St	42 B2
Gibbs Entry	43 E3
Gibson St	46 D4
Gibson Ter	42 A4
Gifford Pk	43 E4
Giles St	47 E3
Gillespie Cres	42 B4
Gillespie Pl	42 B4
Gillespie St	42 B4
Gillsland Pk	49 G6
Gillsland Rd	49 G6
Gilmore Pk	42 A4
Gilmore Pl	49 H5
Gilmore Pl La	42 B4
Gilmour's Entry 7	43 E3
Gilmour St	43 E3
Gladstone Pl	47 G4
Gladstone Ter	50 D5
Glanville Pl 5	46 A6
Glencairn Cres	49 G3
Glendevon Av	48 C4
Glendevon Gdns	48 C4
Glendevon Gro	48 C4
Glendevon Pk	48 C5
Glendevon Pl	48 C4
Glendevon Rd	48 C5
Glendevon Ter	48 C4
Glenfinlas St	42 B2
Glengyle Ter	42 B4
Glenlea Cotts	48 D6
Glenlee Av	51 H2
Glenlee Gdns	51 H2
Glenogle Ct	46 A5
Glenogle Pl 7	46 A5
Glenogle Rd	46 A6
Glenogle Ter	46 A5
Glenorchy Pl 4	43 E1
Glenorchy Ter	51 E6
Glen St	42 C3
Gloucester La	42 B1
Gloucester Pl	42 B1
Gloucester Sq	42 B1
Gloucester St	42 B1
Goldenacre Ter	46 A4
Gordon St	47 F4
Gorgie Cotts	48 D6
Gorgie Pk Cl	49 E6
Gorgie Pk Rd	49 E5
Gorgie Rd	49 E5
Gosford Pl	46 C3
Graham St	46 D3
Grandfield	46 B3
Grandville	46 B2
Grange Ct	50 D5
Grange Cres	50 C6
Grange Ln	50 B6
Grange Ln Gdns	50 C6
Grange Rd	50 C5
Granton Cres	45 G2
Granton Gdns	45 G2
Granton Gro	45 G2
Granton Mains Av	44 D2
Granton Mains Bk 1	44 D2
Granton Mains Brae	44 D2
Granton Mains Ct	45 E2
Granton Mains E	45 E2
Granton Mains Gait	44 D2
Granton Mains Vale	44 D2
Granton Mains Wynd	44 D2
Granton Medway	45 F2
Granton Mill Cres	44 D2
Granton Mill Dr	44 D2
Granton Mill March	44 C3
Granton Mill Pk	44 C3
Granton Mill Pl	44 C2
Granton Mill Rd	44 C2
Granton Mill W 1	44 C2
Granton Pk Av	45 F1
Granton Pl	45 G2
Granton Rd	45 G2
Granton Sq	45 G1
Granton Ter	45 G2
Granton Vw	45 G1
Grantully Pl	51 E6
Granville Ter	49 H5
Grassmarket	42 C3
Grays Ct 6	43 E3
Gray's Ln	49 F6
Great Junct St	47 E3
Great King St	42 C1
Great Michael Cl 4	46 C1
Great Michael Ri	46 C2
Great Michael Sq 1	46 C1
Great Stuart St	42 A2
Green, The	44 A4
Greendale Pk	44 B4
Greenhill Ct	50 A5
Greenhill Gdns	50 A5
Greenhill Pk	50 A6
Greenhill Pl	50 A6
Greenhill Ter	50 A6
Greenside End 6	43 E1
Greenside La	43 E1
Greenside Pl 5	43 E1
Greenside Row	43 E1
Green St	46 C6
Greyfriars Pl	43 D3
Grierson Av	45 H2
Grierson Cres	45 H2
Grierson Gdns	45 H2
Grierson Rd	45 G2
Grierson Sq	45 H2
Grierson Vil	45 H2
Grigor Av	45 E5
Grigor Dr	45 E5
Grigor Gdns	45 E5
Grigor Ter	45 E5
Grindlay St	42 B3
Grindlay St Ct	42 B3
Groathill Av	44 D6
Groathill Gdns E	44 D6
Groathill Gdns W	44 D6
Groathill Ln	44 D5
Groathill Rd N	44 D5
Groathill Rd S	44 D6
Grosvenor Cres	49 G3
Grosvenor Gdns	49 G3
Grosvenor St	42 A3
Grove St	42 A3
Grove Ter 4	42 A3
Guardianswood	48 D3
Gullan's Cl	43 E2
Gunnet Ct	44 B3
Guthrie St	43 D3
Gypsy Brae	44 C2

H

Name	Ref
Haddington Pl	46 D6
Haddon's Ct	43 E3
Hailes St	42 B4
Halmyre St	47 E5
Hamburgh Pl 1	46 D2
Hamilton Pl	46 A6
Hamilton's Folly Ms 5	43 E4
Hamilton Wynd	46 D2
Hammermen's Entry	43 E2
Hampton Pl 4	49 F3
Hampton Ter	49 F3
Hanover St	42 C1
Harden Pl	49 G5
Hardwell Cl	43 E4
Harrismith Pl	47 F6
Harrison Gdns	49 F6
Harrison La	49 G5
Harrison Pl	49 F6
Harrison Rd	49 F6
Hartington Gdns	49 H5
Hartington Pl	49 H5
Hart St	46 C6
Hart St La	46 C6
Hatton Pl	50 C5
Haugh St	46 A6
Hawkhill	47 F5
Hawkhill Av	47 F5
Hawkhill Cl	47 F5
Hawkhill Ct	47 G5
Hawthornbank La	42 A2
Hawthornbank Pl	46 D2
Hawthornbank Ter 2	46 D2
Hawthorn Bldgs 2	49 G2
Hawthornden Pl	46 D5
Hawthorn Ter 5	42 A2
Hawthornvale	46 C2
Haymarket	42 A3
Haymarket Ter	49 G3
Haymarket Yards	49 G3
Hazelbank Ter	49 F6
Henderland Rd	49 E3
Henderson Gdns 4	47 E3
Henderson Pl	46 B6
Henderson Pl La	46 A6
Henderson Row	46 A6
Henderson St	47 E3
Henderson Ter	49 G5
Heriot Br	42 C3
Heriot Cross 1	42 C3
Heriot Hill Ter	46 B5
Heriot Pl	42 C3
Heriot Row	42 B1
Hermand Cres	49 E6
Hermand St	49 E6
Hermand Ter	49 E6
Hermitage Pk	47 F5
Hermitage Pk Gro	47 G5
Hermitage Pk Lea	47 G5
Hermitage Pk S	47 G5
Hermitage Pl	47 F4
Hermits Cft	43 F4
High Riggs	42 C3
High Sch Yards	43 E3
High St	43 D2
Hillend Pl 10	51 H1
Hillhouse Rd	44 A5
Hillpark Av	44 A5
Hillpark Brae	48 A1
Hillpark Ct	44 A5
Hillpark Cres	44 A6
Hillpark Dr	44 A5
Hillpark Gdns	44 A6
Hillpark Grn	44 A6
Hillpark Gro	44 A6
Hillpark Ln	44 B6
Hillpark Rd	44 A6
Hillpark Ter	44 A6
Hillpark Way	44 B6
Hillpark Wd	44 B6
Hill Pl	43 E3
Hillside Cres	46 D6
Hillside St	47 E6
Hill Sq	43 E3
Hill St	42 B1
Hill St La N	42 B1
Hill St La S	42 C2
Hillview	44 C6
Hollybank Ter	49 F6
Holyrood Ct	43 F2
Holyrood Pk	51 F2
Holyrood Pk Rd	51 E5
Holyrood Rd	43 E2
Home St	42 B4
Hopefield Ter	46 D2
Hope Pk Cres	43 E4
Hope Pk Sq 1	43 E4
Hope Pk Ter	43 E4
Hope St	42 B2
Hope St La	42 B2
Hope Ter	50 B6
Hopetoun Cres	46 D6
Hopetoun St	46 D6
Horne Ter	42 A4
Horse Wynd	43 F2
House o'Hill Av	44 B5
House o'Hill Brae	44 B5
House o'Hill Cres	44 B5
House o'Hill Gdns	44 C5
House o'Hill Grn	44 C5
House o'Hill Gro	44 B5
House o'Hill Pl	44 B5
House o'Hill Rd	44 B5
House o'Hill Row	44 C5
House o'Hill Ter	44 C6
Howard Pl	46 B5
Howard St	46 B5
Howden St	43 E3
Howe St	42 C1
Hugh Miller Pl	46 A6
Hunter's Cl 13	42 C3
Hunter Sq	43 D2
Huntingdon Pl	46 D6
Huntly St	46 B5
Hutchison Crossway	48 D6
Hutchison Ho	49 E6
Hutchison Medway	49 E6
Hutchison Pk	48 D6
Hutchison Rd	49 E6
Hutchison Vw	48 D6
Hutton Cl	43 F2
Hutton Rd	43 F2

I

Name	Ref
Imperial Dock	47 F1
Inchcolm Ct	44 D3
Inchgarvie Ct	45 E4
Inchkeith Ct	46 D5
Inchmickery Ct	44 B3
India Bldgs 3	43 D3
India Pl	42 B1
India St	42 B1
Industrial Rd	47 F4
Industry Home 1	46 D3
Industry La	46 D3
Infirmary St	43 E3
Inglis Ct 2	42 C3
Inverleith Av	46 A4
Inverleith Av S	46 A4
Inverleith Gdns	45 H4
Inverleith Gro	45 G5
Inverleith Pl	45 H4
Inverleith Pl La	46 A4
Inverleith Row	46 A4
Inverleith Ter	46 A5
Inverleith Ter La	46 A5
Iona St	47 E5
Iona St La	47 E5
Ivy Ter	49 F5

J

Name	Ref
Jackson's Entry 7	43 F2
Jamaica Ms	42 B1
Jamaica St	42 B1
Jamaica St N La	42 B1
Jamaica St S La	42 B1
Jamaica St W 2	42 B1
James' Ct 4	43 D2
James Craig Wk	43 D1
Jameson Pl	47 E5
Jane St	47 E4
Jane Ter 2	51 F1
Jawbone Wk	43 D4
Jeffrey Av	48 C1
Jeffrey St	43 D2
Jessfield Ter	46 C2
John Cotton Business Cen	47 F6
John's La	47 F3
John's Pl	47 F4
Johnston Ter	42 C3
Junction Pl	47 E4

K

Name	Ref
Keir St	42 C3
Keith Cres	48 C1
Keith Row	48 D1
Keith Ter	48 D1
Kemp Pl	46 A6
Kenmure Av	51 H2
Kerr St	46 A6
Kew Ter	49 F3
Kilgraston Ct	50 B6
Kilgraston Rd	50 C6
Kilmaurs Rd	51 F6
Kilmaurs Ter	51 F6
Kincaid's Ct	43 D3
Kinellan Gdns	48 D3
Kinellan Rd	48 D2
Kinghorn Pl	46 C3
King's Br	42 C3
Kingsburgh Rd	48 D3
Kings Haugh	51 H6
King's Meadow	51 G6
King's Stables La	42 C3
King's Stables Rd	42 C3
King St	47 E3
Kinnear Rd	45 G4
Kirkgate	47 F3
Kirkhill Dr	51 F6
Kirkhill Gdns	51 F5
Kirkhill Rd	51 F5
Kirkhill Ter	51 F5
Kirk St	47 E4
Kirkwood Pl 3	51 F1
Kittle Yards	50 D5
Kyle Pl	43 F1

L

Name	Ref
Ladehead	46 C4
Lady Lawson St	42 C3
Lady Menzies Pl	51 F1
Lady Stair's Cl 6	43 D2
Lady Wynd	42 C3
Lamb's Cl 2	43 E4
Lamb's Ct 1	46 D1
Lansdowne Cres	49 G3
Lapicide Pl	46 D3
Largo Pl	46 D3
Lauderdale St	50 B5
Lauder Ln	50 D6
Lauder Rd	50 C5
Laurel Ter 1	49 F5
Laurie St	47 F4
Lauriston Gdns	42 C3
Lauriston Pk	42 C3
Lauriston Pl	42 B4
Lauriston St	42 C3
Lauriston Ter	42 C3
Laverockbank Av	46 B2
Laverockbank Cres	46 B2
Laverockbank Gdns	46 B2
Laverockbank Gro	46 B2
Laverockbank Rd	46 B2
Laverockbank Ter	46 B2
Lawnmarket	43 D2
Leamington La	50 A5
Leamington Pl	50 A5
Leamington Rd	42 A4
Leamington Ter	42 B4
Learmonth Av	45 G6
Learmonth Ct	49 G1
Learmonth Cres	49 G1
Learmonth Gdns	49 G1
Learmonth Gdns La	49 G1
Learmonth Gdns Ms	45 H6

Learmonth Gro	45 G6
Learmonth Pk	45 G6
Learmonth Pl	45 G6
Learmonth Ter	45 G6
Learmonth Ter La	49 G1
Learmonth Vw 1	42 A1
Leith Docks	47 E1
Leith Links	47 F4
Leith St	43 D1
Leith Wk	46 D6
Lennel Av	48 D2
Lennox Row	46 A2
Lennox St	42 A1
Lennox St La	42 A1
Leopold Pl	46 D6
Leslie Pl	45 H6
Leven Cl 1	42 B4
Leven St	42 B4
Leven Ter	42 C4
Lewis Ter 12	42 A3
Liddesdale Pl	46 A5
Lilyhill Ter	51 H1
Lily Ter 1	49 F6
Limes, The	49 H6
Lindean Pl	47 G4
Lindsay Pl	46 D2
Lindsay Rd	46 C1
Lindsay St	46 D2
Links Gdns	47 G3
Links Gdns La	47 G3
Links La 3	47 F3
Links Pl	47 F3
Linksview Ho	47 F3
Lismore Av	51 H1
Lismore Cres	51 H1
Little King St	43 D1
Livingstone Pl	50 C5
Lixmount Av	46 B2
Lixmount Gdns	46 B2
Loaning Mills	47 H6
Loaning Rd	47 H6
Lochend Av	47 G6
Lochend Castle Barns	47 G6
Lochend Cl	43 F2
Lochend Cres	47 H6
Lochend Dr	47 G6
Lochend Gdns	47 G6
Lochend Gro	47 H6
Lochend Pk	47 G6
Lochend Quad	47 H6
Lochend Rd	47 G5
Lochend Rd S	47 G6
Lochend Sq	47 G6
Lochinvar Dr	45 G1
Lochrin Bldgs	42 B4
Lochrin Pl	42 B4
Lochrin Ter 3	42 B4
Loch Rd	44 B6
Lochview Ct	43 F2
Loganlea Dr	51 H1
Loganlea Gdns	47 H6
Logan St	46 B6
Logie Grn Gdns	46 B5
Logie Grn Ln	46 B5
Logie Grn Rd	46 B5
Logie Mill	46 B5
Lomond Rd	46 A2
London Rd	43 E1
London St	46 C6
Long Craig Rigg	44 D1
Long Craig Rd	44 D1
Lonsdale Ter	42 C4
Lord Russell Pl 1	50 D5
Lorne Pl	47 E5
Lorne Sq	47 E5
Lorne St	47 E5
Lothian Rd	42 B2
Lothian St	43 D3
Lovers' Ln	50 C5
Lower Gilmore Pl	42 A4
Lower Granton Rd	44 A1
Lower London Rd	51 F1
Lufra Bk	45 H2
Lutton Pl	43 E4
Lynedoch Pl	42 A2
Lynedoch Pl La	42 A2
Lyne St	51 F1

M

McDonald Pl	46 C5
McDonald Rd	46 C5
McDonald St	46 D5
McKelvie Par	46 A1
Mackenzie Pl	42 B1
McLaren Rd	51 F6
McLaren Ter 11	42 A3
McLeod St	49 F4
McNeill St	42 A4
Madeira Pl	46 D3
Madeira St	46 D2
Magdala Cres	49 G3
Magdala Ms	49 G3
Maidencraig Ct	44 D6
Maidencraig Cres	44 D6
Maidencraig Gro	44 D6
Main Pt	42 C3
Main St	44 A5
Malta Grn 2	46 A6
Malta Ter	46 A6
Manderston St	47 E4
Manor Pl	42 A2
Mansfield Pl	46 C6
Mansionhouse Rd	50 C5
Marchfield Gro	44 B5
Marchfield Pk	44 A5
Marchfield Pk La	44 A5
Marchfield Ter	44 B6
March Gait	44 A6
March Gro	44 A6
Marchhall Cres	51 F5
Marchhall Pl	51 F5
Marchhall Rd	51 F5
Marchmont Cres	50 B5
Marchmont Rd	50 B5
Marchmont St	50 B5
March Pines	44 A6
March Rd	44 A6
Mardale Cres	49 H6
Marine Dr	44 B2
Marine Esplanade	47 H3
Marionville Av	47 G6
Marionville Cres	47 H6
Marionville Dr	47 H6
Marionville Gro	47 H6
Marionville Medway 1	47 H6
Marionville Pk	47 G6
Marionville Rd	51 F1
Marischal Pl 1	48 D1
Maritime La	47 F3
Maritime St	47 F3
Market St	43 D2
Marshall's Ct 3	43 E1
Marshall St 2	43 E3
Martello Ct	44 B3
Maryfield	43 F1
Maryfield Pl	51 F1
Mary's Pl 1	45 H6
May Ct	44 B3
Mayfield Gdns	51 E6
Mayfield Gdns La	51 E6
Mayfield Rd	51 E6
Mayfield Ter	51 E6
Mayville Gdns	46 B2
Mayville Gdns E	46 B2
Meadowbank	51 G1
Meadowbank Av	51 G1
Meadowbank Cres	51 G1
Meadowbank Ho	51 H1
Meadowbank Pl 7	51 H1
Meadowbank Shop Pk	47 F6
Meadowbank Ter	51 G1
Meadow La	43 D4
Meadow Pl	42 C4
Meadow Pl La	50 C5
Melbourne Pl 7	43 D2
Melgund Ter	46 C6
Melville Cres	42 A2
Melville Dr	42 C4
Melville Pl 6	42 A2
Melville St	42 A2
Melville St La	42 A2
Melville Ter	50 C5
Mentone Gdns	51 E6
Merchant St	43 D3
Merchiston Av	49 H5
Merchiston Bk Av	49 H6
Merchiston Bk Gdns	49 H6
Merchiston Cres	49 H6
Merchiston Gro	49 H6
Merchiston Ms	49 H5
Merchiston Pk	49 H5
Merchiston Pl	49 H6
Mertoun Pl	49 G5
Meuse La	43 D2
Middleby St	51 E6
Middlefield	46 D5
Middle Meadow Wk	43 D4
Middle Pier	45 G1
Mid Gillsland Rd	49 G6
Millerfield Pl	50 C5
Miller Row	42 A2
Mill La	47 E3
Milnacre	46 C4
Milton St	51 F1
Minto St	51 E5
Mitchell St	47 F3
Moat Dr	49 E6
Moat Ho	49 E6
Moat Pl	49 E6
Moat St	49 E6
Moat Ter	49 E6
Moncrieff Ter	50 D5
Monkwood Ct	50 C6
Monmouth Ter	46 A3
Montague St	43 E4
Montagu Ter	46 A4
Montgomery St	46 D6
Montgomery St La	46 D6
Montpelier	49 H5
Montpelier Pk	49 H5
Montpelier Ter	49 H5
Montrose Ter	43 F1
Moray Pk	51 F1
Moray Pk Ter	51 F1
Moray Pl	42 B1
Morningside Rd	49 H6
Morrison Circ	42 A3
Morrison Cres	42 A3
Morrison Link	42 A3
Morrison St	42 A3
Moston Ter	51 E6
Mound, The	42 C2
Mound Pl	42 C2
Mount Gra	50 B6
Muirdale Ter 1	44 C6
Muirhouse Av	44 C4
Muirhouse Av N	44 C3
Muirhouse Bk	44 C4
Muirhouse Cl	44 B4
Muirhouse Cres	44 C3
Muirhouse Dr	44 B3
Muirhouse Gdns	44 B3
Muirhouse Grn	44 B3
Muirhouse Gro	44 B3
Muirhouse Ln	44 C3
Muirhouse Medway	44 B3
Muirhouse Pk	44 B4
Muirhouse Parkway	44 C3
Muirhouse Pl E	44 C4
Muirhouse Pl W	44 C4
Muirhouse Ter	44 B4
Muirhouse Vw	44 B3
Muirhouse Way	44 C4
Mulberry Pl 1	46 C3
Multrees Wk	43 D1
Munro Pl 1	46 B5
Murano Pl	47 E6
Murdoch Ter	42 A4
Murieston Cres	49 F4
Murieston Cres La 2	49 G4
Murieston La	49 F4
Murieston Pl	49 F4
Murieston Rd	49 F4
Murieston Ter	49 F4
Murrayfield Av	49 E3
Murrayfield Dr	48 D3
Murrayfield Gdns	49 E2
Murrayfield Pl 1	49 E3
Murrayfield Rd	48 D2
Myrtle Ter	49 F5

N

Napier Ln	49 G6
Napier Rd	49 G6
Nelson Pl 1	42 C1
Nelson St	42 C1
Nether Bakehouse 9	43 F2
Netherby Rd	45 H3
Nether Craigwell	43 F2
New Arthur Pl	43 E3
New Arthur St 5	43 E3
Newbattle Ter	50 A6
New Bells Ct 4	47 F3
New Broompark	45 F1
New Broughton	46 C6
New Cut Rigg	45 F1
Newhaven Main St	46 B1
Newhaven Pl	46 C1
Newhaven Rd	46 C2
Newington Rd	50 D5
New John's Pl	43 E4
Newkirkgate 2	47 E4
Newlands Pk	51 E6
New La	46 C2
New Orchardfield	47 E4
New Skinner's Cl	43 E2
News Steps	43 D2
New St	43 E2
Newton St	49 F5
Nicholfield	46 C2
Nicolson Sq	43 D3
Nicolson St	43 E3
Niddry St	43 D2
Niddry St S 3	43 E3
Nisbet Ct	47 G5
Noble Pl	47 G4
North Bk St	43 D2
North Br	43 D2
North Br Arc 10	43 D2
North Castle St	42 B1
North Charlotte St	42 B1
North Clyde St La 1	43 D1
Northcote St	49 G4
North E Circ Pl	42 B1
North Fort St	46 D2
North Hillhousefield	46 D2
North Junct St	46 D2
North Leith Mill 4	46 D2
North Leith Sands	46 D2
North Meadow Wk	42 C4
North Pk Ter	45 H6
North Richmond St 1	43 E3
North St. Andrew La	43 D1
North St. Andrew St	43 D1
North St. David St	43 D1
Northumberland Pl 2	42 C1
Northumberland Pl La	42 C1
Northumberland St	42 C1
Northumberland St N E La	42 C1
Northumberland St N W La	42 C1
Northumberland St S E La	42 C1
Northumberland St S W La	42 C1
Northview Ct	44 C3
North Werber Pk	45 F5
North Werber Pl	45 F4
North Werber Rd	45 F5
North W Circ Pl	42 B1
Norton Pk	47 F6

O

Oakfield Pl	43 E3
Oakville Ter	47 G4
Ocean Dr	46 D2
Ocean Terminal Shop Cen	46 D1
Ogilvie Ter	49 F6
Old Assembly Cl 9	43 D2
Old Broughton 2	46 C6
Old Ch La	51 H4
Old Fishmarket Cl	43 D2
Old Tolbooth Wynd	43 E2
Orchard Bk	49 F1
Orchard Brae	45 G6
Orchard Brae Av	49 F1
Orchard Brae Gdns	49 F1
Orchard Brae Gdns W	49 F1
Orchard Brae W	45 G6
Orchard Cres	49 E1
Orchard Dr	49 E1
Orchardfield La	47 E5
Orchard Gro	45 G6
Orchard Pl	45 F6
Orchard Rd	49 F1
Orchard Rd S	49 E1
Orchard Ter	49 F1
Orchard Toll	49 F1
Ormidale Ter	48 D3
Orwell Pl	49 G4
Orwell Ter	49 G4
Osborne Ter	49 G3
Oxcars Ct	44 B3
Oxcraig St	45 G1
Oxford St	43 F4
Oxford Ter	42 A1

P

Paisley Cres	51 H2
Paisley Gdns	51 H2
Paisley Ter	51 H2
Palmerston Pl	42 A2
Palmerston Pl La	42 A3
Palmerston Rd	50 C5
Panmure Pl	42 C4
Papermill Wynd	46 D5
Pape's Cotts	49 E3
Park Pl	46 B2
Park Rd	46 B2
Parkside St	43 F4
Parkside Ter	43 F4
Parkvale Pl	47 G4
Parliament Sq	43 D2
Parliament St	47 F3
Parsons Grn Ter 2	51 H1
Patrick Geddes Steps 14	42 C3
Patriothall 3	46 A6
Pattison St	47 F3
Peacock Ct	46 C1
Peel Ter	51 E6
Peffermill Ind Est	51 H6
Pembroke Pl	49 F3
Pennywell Cotts	44 C2
Pennywell Ct	44 C3
Pennywell Gdns	44 B3
Pennywell Gro	44 C3
Pennywell Medway	44 B3
Pennywell Pl	44 C3
Pennywell Rd	44 C3
Pennywell Vil	44 D2
Persevere Ct	47 E2

EDINBURGH

Name	Ref	Name	Ref
Perth St	46 A6	Quayside Mills 3	47 E3
Picardy Pl	43 E1	Quayside St	47 E3
Pier Pl	46 B1	Queen Charlotte La	47 F3
Piershill La 3	51 H1	Queen Charlotte St	47 F3
Piershill Pl 4	51 H1	Queen's Av	44 C6
Piershill Sq W	51 H1	Queen's Av S	44 D6
Pilrig Cotts	47 E5	Queen's Cres	51 E6
Pilrig Gdns	46 D4	Queen's Dr	43 F3
Pilrig Glebe	47 E5	Queensferry Rd	49 G1
Pilrig Hts	46 C4	Queensferry St	42 A2
Pilrig Ho Cl	46 D4	Queensferry St La	42 A2
Pilrig Ind Est	46 D4	Queensferry Ter	49 F1
Pilrig Pl	47 E5	Queen's Gdns	44 D6
Pilrig St	46 D4	Queen's Pk Av	51 G1
Pilton Av	45 E3	Queen's Pk Ct	51 H2
Pilton Cres	45 G3	Queen's Rd	44 D6
Pilton Dr	45 F3	Queen St	42 B1
Pilton Dr N	45 F2	Queen St Gdns E	42 C1
Pilton Gdns	45 F3	Queen St Gdns W	42 C1
Pilton Ln	45 F3	Quilts, The	46 D3
Pilton Pk	45 F3	Quilts Wynd	46 D3
Pilton Pl	45 F3		
Pinkhill	48 A4	**R**	
Pirniefield Bk	47 H4	Raeburn Ms	45 H6
Pirniefield Gdns	47 H4	Raeburn Pl	45 H6
Pirniefield Gro	47 H4	Raeburn St	45 H6
Pirniefield Pl	47 H4	Ramsay Gdn	42 C2
Pirniefield Ter	47 H4	Ramsay La	42 C2
Pirrie St	47 E4	Randolph Cliff	42 A2
Pitlochry Pl	47 F6	Randolph Cres	42 A2
Pitsligo Rd	50 A6	Randolph La	42 B2
Pitt St	46 C3	Randolph Pl	42 B2
Playfair Steps 1	42 C2	Rankeillor St	43 E4
Pleasance	43 E3	Ratcliffe Ter	50 D5
Pollard Glebe	48 B6	Ravelston Ct	49 E2
Polwarth Cres	49 H5	Ravelston Dykes	49 E2
Polwarth Gdns	49 G6	Ravelston Dykes La	48 B2
Polwarth Gro	49 G6	Ravelston Dykes Rd	48 C1
Polwarth Pk	49 G5	Ravelston Gdn	48 D2
Polwarth Pl	49 G5	Ravelston Hts	48 D1
Polwarth Ter	49 G6	Ravelston Ho Gro	48 D1
Ponton St	42 B4	Ravelston Ho Ln	48 D1
Poplar La	47 F3	Ravelston Ho Pk	48 D1
Porterfield Rd	45 F5	Ravelston Ho Rd	48 D1
Portgower Pl	45 H6	Ravelston Pk	49 F2
Port Hamilton	42 B3	Ravelston Pl 4	48 D2
Portland Gdns	46 D2	Ravelston Ri	48 D2
Portland Row	46 D2	Ravelston Ter	48 D1
Portland St	46 D2	Redbraes Gro	46 C4
Portland Ter 3	46 D2	Redbraes Pl	46 C4
Portsburgh Sq 5	42 C3	Reekie's Ct	43 E3
Potterrow	43 D3	Regent Br 2	43 D1
Powderhall Brae	46 C4	Regent Pl	51 F1
Powderhall Rigg	46 C4	Regent Rd	43 E1
Powderhall Rd	46 C5	Regent's Ct 1	49 G4
Prestonfield Av	51 F6	Regent Ter	43 E1
Prestonfield Bk	51 F6	Regent Ter Ms	43 F1
Prestonfield Cres	51 F6	Register Pl	43 D1
Prestonfield Gdns	51 F6	Reid's Cl	43 F2
Prestonfield Rd	51 F6	Reid's Ct 1	43 F2
Prestonfield Ter	51 F6	Reid Ter	45 H6
Priestfield Av	51 G6	Rennie's Isle	47 E2
Priestfield Cres	51 G6	Restalrig Av	51 H1
Priestfield Gdns	51 G6	Restalrig Circ	47 H5
Priestfield Gro	51 F5	Restalrig Cres	47 H5
Priestfield Rd	51 F6	Restalrig Dr	47 H6
Priestfield Rd N	51 F5	Restalrig Gdns	47 H6
Primrose Bk Rd	46 A2	Restalrig Pk	47 G5
Primrose St	47 F4	Restalrig Rd	47 G4
Primrose Ter	49 F5	Restalrig Rd S	51 H1
Prince of Wales Dock	47 E1	Restalrig Sq	47 H5
Prince Regent St	46 D2	Restalrig Ter	47 F4
Princes Mall	43 D2	Richmond La	43 E3
Princes St	42 C2	Richmond Pl	43 E3
Prospect Bk Cres	47 G4	Richmond Ter	42 A3
Prospect Bk Gdns	47 G5	Riego St	42 B3
Prospect Bk Gro	47 H4	Rillbank Cres	50 C5
Prospect Bk Pl	47 H4	Rillbank Ter	50 C5
Prospect Bk Rd	47 G4	Rintoul Pl	46 A6
Prospect Bk Ter	47 H4	Ritchie Pl	49 G5
		Riversdale Cres	48 D4
Q		Riversdale Gro	48 D3
Quality St	44 A5		
Quality St La	44 A5		
Quarry Cl	43 E4		

Name	Ref	Name	Ref	Name	Ref
Riversdale Rd	48 C3	St. Anthony St 6	47 E3	Saunders St	42 A6
Robb's Ln	48 D6	St. Bernard's Cres	42 A1	Saxe-Coburg Pl	46 A6
Robb's Ln Gro	48 D6	St. Bernard's Row	46 A6	Saxe-Coburg St	46 A6
Robertson Av	49 E5	St. Catherine's Gdns	48 B4	Saxe-Coburg Ter 4	46 A6
Robertson Gait	49 E6	St. Catherine's Pl	50 D5	Sciennes	50 D5
Robertson's Cl	43 E3	St. Clair Av	47 F5	Sciennes Gdns	50 D5
Robertson's Ct 2	43 F2	St. Clair Pl	47 F5	Sciennes Hill Pl	50 D5
Rocheid Ms	45 G4	St. Clair Rd	47 F5	Sciennes Ho Pl	50 D5
Rocheid Path	46 A5	St. Clair St	47 F5	Sciennes Pl 2	50 D5
Rochester Ter	49 H6	St. Colme St	42 B2	Sciennes Rd	50 C5
Rodney Pl	46 B6	St. David's Pl 9	42 A3	Scone Gdns	51 H1
Rodney St	46 B5	St. David's Ter 10	42 A3	Scotland St	46 B6
Romero Pl	51 E5	St. Giles' St	43 D2	Seacot 1	47 H4
Ronaldson's Wf	47 E3	St. James Cen	43 D1	Seafield Av	47 H4
Rosebank Cotts	42 A3	St. James' Pl	43 D1	Seafield Pl	47 H4
Rosebank Gdns	45 H3	St. James Sq	43 D1	Seafield Rd	47 H4
Rosebank Gro	45 H3	St. John's Cres	48 A4	Seaforth Dr	44 D6
Rosebank Rd	45 H3	St. John's Hill 9	43 E3	Seaforth Ter	44 D6
Rosebery Cres	49 G3	St. John St	43 E2	Sealcarr St	45 F1
Rosebery Cres La	49 G3	St. Leonard's Bk	43 F4	Seaport St 5	47 F3
Roseburn Av	49 E3	St. Leonard's Crag 1	43 F4	Semple St	42 B3
Roseburn Cliff	49 E3	St. Leonard's Hill	43 E4	Seton Pl	50 D5
Roseburn Cres	49 E4	St. Leonard's La	43 E4	Shaftesbury Pk	49 F6
Roseburn Dr	49 E3	St. Leonard's St	43 E4	Shandon Cres	49 F6
Roseburn Gdns 2	49 E3	St. Margaret's Pl	50 B6	Shandon Pl	49 F6
Roseburn Maltings	49 F3	St. Margaret's Rd	50 A6	Shandon Rd	49 F6
Roseburn Pl	49 E3	St. Mary's St	43 E2	Shandon St	49 F6
Roseburn St	49 E4	St. Ninian's Row 3	43 D1	Shandon Ter	49 F6
Roseburn Ter	49 E4	St. Patrick Sq	43 E4	Shandwick Pl	42 A3
Rosemount Bldgs	42 A3	St. Patrick St 3	43 E4	Shaw's Pl	46 D5
Roseneath Pl	50 B5	St. Peter's Bldgs	42 A4	Shaw's Sq 2	46 D6
Roseneath St	50 C5	St. Peter's Pl	42 A4	Shaw's St	46 D5
Roseneath Ter	50 C5	St. Stephen Pl	46 A6	Shaw's Ter	46 D5
Rose Pk	46 A3	St. Stephen St	46 A6	Sheriff Bk	47 E3
Rose St	42 B2	St. Teresa Pl	49 G6	Sheriff Brae	47 E3
Rose St N La	42 B2	St. Thomas Rd	50 C6	Sheriff Pk	47 E3
Rose St S La	42 B2	St. Triduana's Rest	47 H6	Shore	47 F3
Rosevale Pl 1	47 G4	St. Vincent Pl	46 A6	Shore Pl	47 F3
Rosevale Ter	47 F4	St. Vincent St	46 B6	Shrub Pl	46 D5
Roseville Gdns	46 B2	Salamander Ct	47 G3	Shrub Pl La	46 D5
Rossie Pl	47 E6	Salamander Pl	47 G3	Sienna Gdns	50 D5
Rosslyn Cres	46 D5	Salamander St	47 F3	Silverknowes Bk	44 A4
Rosslyn Ter	46 D5	Salamander Yards	47 H4	Silverknowes Brae	44 A4
Rothesay Ms	49 G2	Salisbury Ms	51 E5	Silverknowes Ct	44 A4
Rothesay Pl	49 G2	Salisbury Pl	50 D5	Silverknowes Cres	44 A3
Rothesay Ter	49 G2	Salisbury Rd	51 E5	Silverknowes Dell	44 A4
Roxburgh Pl	43 E3	Salmond Pl	47 F6	Silverknowes Dr	44 A4
Roxburgh St	43 E3	Salvesen Cres	44 B2	Silverknowes Eastway	44 A4
Royal Circ	42 B1	Salvesen Gdns	44 C2	Silverknowes Gdns	44 A3
Royal Cres	46 B6	Salvesen Gro	44 C2	Silverknowes Grn	44 B4
Royal Pk Pl	51 G1	Salvesen Ter	44 C2	Silverknowes Gro	44 A3
Royal Pk Ter	51 G1	Sand Port	47 E2	Silverknowes Hill	44 A4
Royal Ter	43 E1	Sandport Pl	47 E2	Silverknowes Midway	44 B4
Royal Ter Ms	43 F1	Sandport St	47 E2	Silverknowes Neuk	44 B5
Royston Mains Av	45 E2	Sandport Way	47 E3	Silverknowes Parkway	44 A3
Royston Mains Cl	45 F2	Sauchiebank	49 F4	Silverknowes Pl	44 A3
Royston Mains Cres	45 E2	Saughton Av	48 D5	Silverknowes Rd	44 A3
Royston Mains Gdns	45 F2	Saughton Cres	48 C4	Silverknowes Rd E	44 A4
Royston Mains Grn	45 F2	Saughton Gdns	48 C4	Silverknowes Rd S	44 A5
Royston Mains Pl	45 E2	Saughton Gro	48 C4	Silverknowes Southway	44 B4
Royston Mains Rd	45 F2	Saughtonhall Av	48 C4	Silverknowes Vw	44 B4
Royston Mains St	45 E2	Saughtonhall Av W	48 C4	Silvermills	46 A6
Royston Ter	46 A4	Saughtonhall Circ	48 D4	Simon Sq 4	43 E3
Russell Gdns	49 F3	Saughtonhall Cres	48 C4	Sinclair Cl 2	49 F6
Russell Pl	46 A2	Saughtonhall Dr	48 C3	Sinclair Gdns	49 F5
Russell Rd	49 F3	Saughtonhall Gdns	48 D4	Sinclair Pl	49 E5
Rutland Ct 2	42 B3	Saughtonhall Gro	48 D4	Slateford Gait	49 E5
Rutland Ct La	42 B3	Saughtonhall Pl	48 D4	Slateford Grn	49 E5
Rutland Pl 1	42 B2	Saughtonhall Ter	48 D4	Slateford Rd	49 E6
Rutland Sq	42 B2	Saughton Ln	48 C4	Slateford Rd Br	49 E6
Rutland St	42 B2	Saughton Mains Av	48 A6	Slater's Steps 6	43 F2
Ryehill Av	47 G4	Saughton Mains Bk	48 A6	Sleigh Dr	47 H5
Ryehill Gdns	47 G4	Saughton Mains Pk	48 A6	Sleigh Gdns	47 H6
Ryehill Gro	47 G5	Saughton Mains St	48 A6	Sloan St	46 D5
Ryehill Pl	47 G4	Saughton Mains Ter	48 A6	Smithfield St	49 E5
Ryehill Ter	47 G4	Saughton Pk	48 C4	Smith's Pl	47 E4
		Saughton Rd	48 A6	Solicitor's Bldgs 4	43 D3
S				Somerset Pl	47 F4
St. Andrew Pl	47 F4			South Beechwood	48 B4
St. Andrew Sq	43 D1			South Br	43 D2
St. Anthony La	47 E3				
St. Anthony Pl 5	47 E3				

56

South Charlotte St	42	B2
South Clerk St	43	E4
South Coll St	43	D3
South E Circ Pl 1	42	B1
South Ettrick Rd	49	G6
South Fort St	46	D3
South Gayfield La	46	D6
South Gillsand Rd	49	G6
South Gray's Cl	43	E2
South Gray St	51	E6
South Groathill Av	44	D6
South Lauder Rd	50	D6
South Laverockbank Av	46	B2
South Learmonth Av	49	G1
South Learmonth Gdns	49	G1
South Lorne Pl	47	E5
South Meadow Wk	42	C4
South Oxford St	51	E5
South Pk	46	C2
South St. Andrew St	43	D1
South St. David St	43	D1
South Sloan St	47	E5
South Trinity Rd	46	A3
Spencer Pl	46	A2
Spence St	51	E5
Spey St	46	D5
Spey St La	46	D5
Spey Ter	46	D5
Spier's Pl 7	47	E3
Spittalfield Cres	43	E4
Spittal St	42	B3
Spittal St La 3	42	C3
Spottiswoode Rd	50	B5
Spottiswoode St	50	B5
Springfield	46	D4
Springfield Bldgs 3	47	E4
Springfield La	47	E4
Springfield St	47	E4
Spring Gdns	51	F1
Springwell Pl	49	G4
Spylaw Rd	49	G6
Stafford St	42	A2
Stair Pk	48	D3
Stanhope Pl	49	F3
Stanhope St	49	F3
Stanley Pl	51	F1
Stanley Rd	46	B2
Stanwell St	47	E4
Starbank Rd	46	B2
Stead's Pl	47	E4
Stenhouse Av	48	B6
Stenhouse Av W	48	B6
Stenhouse Cotts	48	B6
Stenhouse Cres	48	B6
Stenhouse Cross	48	B6
Stenhouse Dr	48	B6
Stenhouse Gdns	48	B6
Stenhouse Gdns N	48	B6
Stenhouse Gro	48	B6
Stenhouse Pl E	48	B6
Stenhouse Pl W	48	B6
Stenhouse St E	48	B6
Stenhouse St W	48	A6
Stenhouse Ter	48	C6
Stevenlaw's Cl	43	D2
Stevenson Av	48	D5
Stevenson Dr	48	B6
Stevenson Gro	48	D5
Stevenson Rd	48	D5
Stevenson Ter	48	D5
Stewartfield	46	C4
Stewart Ter	49	E5
Stirling Rd	46	A2
Strachan Gdns	44	B6
Strachan Rd	48	C1
Strathearn Pl	50	A6
Strathearn Rd	50	B6
Succoth Av	49	E2
Succoth Ct	49	E2
Succoth Gdns	49	E2
Succoth Pk	48	D2
Succoth Pl	49	E2
Summerbank	46	B6
Summerbank Gdns	47	G4
Summerfield Pl	47	G4
Summerhall 4	50	D5
Summerhall Cres 4	43	E4
Summerhall Pl 5	50	D5
Summerhall Sq	50	D5
Summer Pl	46	B5
Summerside Pl	46	C3
Summerside St	46	C3
Sunbury Ms	49	G2
Sunbury Pl	49	G2
Sunbury St	49	G2
Sunnybank	51	G1
Sunnybank Pl	51	G1
Sunnybank Ter 4	51	F1
Sunnyside	47	F6
Surrey Pl 2	49	F3
Sutherland St	49	F3
Swanfield	47	E3
Sylvan Pl	50	C5

T

Tanfield	46	B5
Tantallon Pl	50	D5
Tarvit St	42	B4
Taylor Gdns	47	E3
Taylor Pl	51	F1
Tay St	49	G5
Telfer Sub	49	G4
Telford Dr	45	E5
Telford Gdns	45	E5
Telford Gro	45	E4
Telford March	45	E5
Telford Pl	45	E5
Telford Rd	45	E6
Temple Pk Cres	49	G5
Tennant St	47	E4
Terrars Cft	43	F4
Teviotdale Pl	46	A6
Teviot Pl	43	D3
Thirlestane La	50	B6
Thirlestane Rd	50	B5
Thistle Ct 3	42	C1
Thistle Pl	42	A4
Thistle St	42	C1
Thistle St N E La	42	C1
Thistle St N W La	42	C1
Thistle St S E La	42	C1
Thistle St S W La	42	C1
Thomson's Ct 8	42	C3
Thorntreeside	47	F4
Thorntree St	47	E4
Thornville Ter	47	F5
Thornybauk	42	B3
Timber Bush	47	F2
Tinto Pl	46	D4
Tipperlinn Rd	49	H6
Tolbooth Wynd	47	F3
Torphichen Pl	42	A3
Torphichen St	42	A3
Tower Pl	47	F2
Tower St	47	F2
Tower St La	47	F2
Tower Wynd	47	F2
Townswomen's Guild Wk	43	D4
Trafalgar La	46	C3
Trafalgar St	46	C3
Traquair Pk E	48	A4
Trinity Ct	46	A3
Trinity Cres	46	A1
Trinity Gro	46	A2
Trinity Mains	46	A3
Trinity Rd	46	A2
Trinity Way	46	A3
Tron Sq 12	43	D2
Tynecastle La	49	F5
Tynecastle Ter	49	F5
Tytler Ct	51	F1
Tytler Gdns	43	F1

U

Ulster Cres	51	H2
Ulster Dr	51	H2
Union Pl 2	43	E1
Union St	46	C6
Upper Bow 8	43	D2
Upper Coltbridge Ter	49	E2
Upper Damside	49	G2
Upper Dean Ter	42	A1
Upper Gilmore Pl	42	B4
Upper Gilmore Ter	42	B4
Upper Gray St	50	D5
Upper Greenside La 7	43	E1
Upper Gro Pl	42	A4
Upper Hermitage	47	F4

V

Valleyfield St	42	B4
Vanburgh Pl	47	F4
Veitch's Sq	46	A6
Vennel	42	C3
Ventnor Pl	51	F6
Ventnor Ter	51	E6
Victoria Dock	47	F2
Victoria Quay	47	E2
Victoria St	43	D3
Victoria Ter 9	43	D3
Viewcraig Gdns	43	E2
Viewcraig St	43	E2
Viewforth	42	A4
Viewforth Gdns	50	A5
Viewforth Sq	49	H5
Viewforth Ter	49	H5
Violet Ter	49	F5
Vivian Ter	44	A5

W

Walker St	42	A2
Walker Ter 6	42	A3
Warden's Cl	43	D3
Wardie Av	45	H3
Wardieburn Dr	45	G2
Wardieburn Pl E	45	G2
Wardieburn Pl N	45	G2
Wardieburn Pl S	45	G2
Wardieburn Pl W	45	F2
Wardieburn Rd	45	G2
Wardieburn St E	45	G2
Wardieburn St W	45	F2
Wardieburn Ter	45	F2
Wardie Cres	45	G2
Wardie Dell	45	H2
Wardiefield	45	G2
Wardie Gro	45	G2
Wardie Ho La	45	H1
Wardie Pk	45	H3
Wardie Rd	45	H3
Wardie Sq	45	H2
Wardie Steps	45	H2
Wardlaw Pl	49	F5
Wardlaw St	49	F5
Wardlaw Ter	49	F5
Warrender Pk Cres	50	A5
Warrender Pk Rd	50	B5
Warrender Pk Ter	50	B5
Warriston Av	46	B4
Warriston Cres	46	B4
Warriston Dr	46	A4
Warriston Gdns	46	A4
Warriston Gro	46	A4
Warriston Pl	46	B4
Warriston Rd	46	B3
Warriston's Cl 15	43	D2
Warriston Ter	46	A4
Washington La	49	G4
Washington St	49	G4
Waterfront Av	45	E1
Waterfront Bdy	45	E1
Waterfront Gate	44	C2
Waterloo Pl	43	D1
Water's Cl 6	47	F3
Water St	47	F3
Watson Cres	49	G5
Waverley Br	43	D2
Waverley Pk	51	F1
Waverley Pk Ter	51	F1
Waverley Pl	51	F1
Waverley St	43	D2
Websters Land 10	42	C3
Well Ct 4	42	A2
Wellington Pl	47	F3
Wellington St	47	E6
Wemyss Pl	42	B1
Wemyss Pl Ms	42	B1
Werberside Ms	45	F4
West Adam St	43	E3
West Annandale St	46	C5
West App Rd	42	B3
West Bow	43	D3
West Bowl Grn St	46	D3
West Bryson Rd	49	G5
West Castle Rd	49	H5
West Catherine Pl	49	F3
West Cherrybank	46	B2
West Coates	49	F3
West Coll St	43	D3
West Ct	48	D1
West Cromwell St 1	47	E2
West Crosscauseway	43	E4
West End	42	B2
West End Pl	49	G4
Wester Cl 3	46	C1
Wester Coates Av	49	F3
Wester Coates Gdns	49	F3
Wester Coates Pl	49	F3
Wester Coates Rd	49	F3
Wester Coates Ter	49	F3
Wester Drylaw Av	44	C5
Wester Drylaw Dr	44	C5
Wester Drylaw Pk	44	D5
Wester Drylaw Pl	44	C5
Wester Drylaw Row	44	D6
Western Cor 1	48	C3
Western Gdns	48	D3
Western Harbour	46	D1
Western Harbour Dr	46	C1
Western Pl	48	D3
Western Ter	48	D3
West Ferryfield	45	G3
Westfield Av	48	D5
Westfield Ct	48	D5
Westfield Rd	49	E5
Westfield St	49	E5
West Fountain Pl	49	G4
West Gorgie Pk	48	D6
West Gra Gdns	50	C6
West Granton Access	45	E2
West Granton Rd	45	F2
Westhall Gdns	50	A5
West Harbour Rd	45	F1
West Maitland St	42	A3
West Mayfield	51	E6
West Mill La	42	A2
West Montgomery Pl	46	D6
West Newington Pl	50	D5
West Nicolson St	43	E3
West Norton Pl	43	F1
West Pk Pl	49	G4
West Pier	45	F1
West Pilton Av	44	C3
West Pilton Bk	44	C3
West Pilton Brae	45	E3
West Pilton Cres	44	C3
West Pilton Crossway	44	D3
West Pilton Dr	44	D3
West Pilton Gdns	44	D3
West Pilton Grn	44	D3
West Pilton Gro	44	D4
West Pilton Lea	44	D3
West Pilton Ln	44	D3
West Pilton March	45	E2
West Pilton Pk	44	D3
West Pilton Pl	44	D3
West Pilton Ri	44	D3
West Pilton Rd	45	E3
West Pilton St	44	D3
West Pilton Ter	44	D3
West Pilton Vw	44	D4
West Pilton Way	45	E3
West Port	42	C3
West Preston St	50	D5
West Register St	43	D1
West Register St La 4	43	D1
West Richmond St	43	E3
West Scotland St La	46	B6
West Shore Business Cen	44	D1
West Shore Rd	44	C2
West Shore Rd Trd Est	44	D1
West Silvermills La	46	A6
West Stanhope Pl 1	49	F3
West Tollcross	42	B4
West Werberside	45	F4
West Winnelstrae	45	G4
West Wds	45	F5
Wheatfield Pl	49	E5
Wheatfield Rd	49	E5
Wheatfield St	49	F5
Wheatfield Ter 1	49	E5
Whitehall Ct	44	C6
White Horse Cl	43	F2
Whitehouse Ln	50	A5
Whitehouse Ter	50	B6
White Pk	49	F5
Whitingford	46	C3
Whitson Cres	48	C5
Whitson Gro	48	C5
Whitson Pl E	48	C5
Whitson Pl W	48	C5
Whitson Rd	48	B5
Whitson Ter	48	C5
Whitson Wk	48	B5
Whitson Way	48	C5
Whyte Pl	51	F1
Wilfrid Ter 5	51	H1
William St	42	A2
William St La N E	42	A2
William St La N W	42	A2
William St La S E	42	A2
William St La S W	42	A2
Willowbank Row	46	C2
Willowbrae Av	51	H2
Willowbrae Rd	51	H2
Wilson's Ct 3	43	E2
Windmill Cl	43	E4
Windmill La	43	D4
Windmill Pl 6	43	E4
Windmill St	43	D4
Windsor St	46	D6
Windsor St La	46	D6
Wishaw Ter	51	G1
Wolseley Cres	51	H1
Wolseley Gdns 8	51	H1
Wolseley Pl 8	51	H1
Wolseley Ter 6	51	H1
Woodbine Ter	47	F5
Woodville Ter	47	F5
Wright's Hos	50	A5
Wyvern Pk	50	C6

Y

Yardheads	47	E3
Yeaman La	49	G4
Yeaman Pl	49	G4
York Bldgs 7	43	D1
York La	43	D1
York Pl	43	D1
York Rd	46	B2
Young St	42	B2
Young St La N	42	B2
Young St La S	42	B2

Z

Zetland Pl	46	A2

EDINBURGH

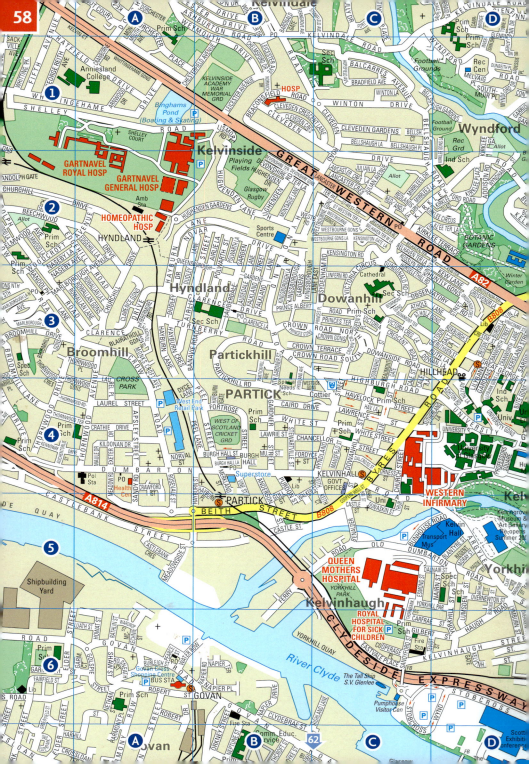

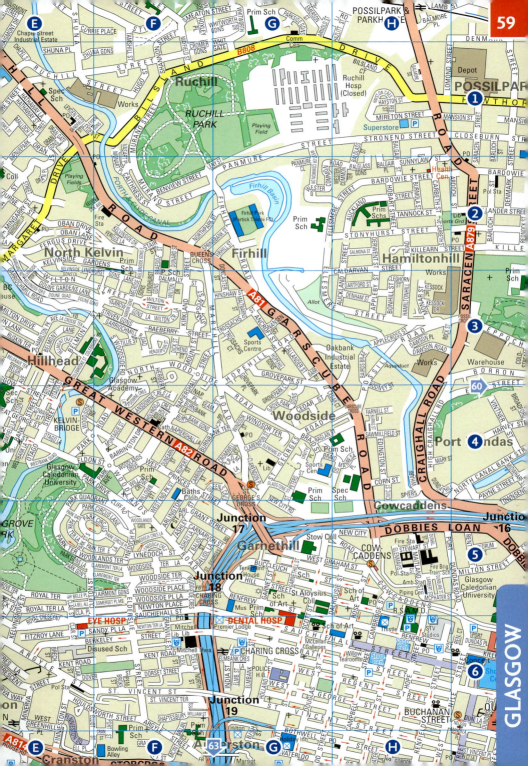

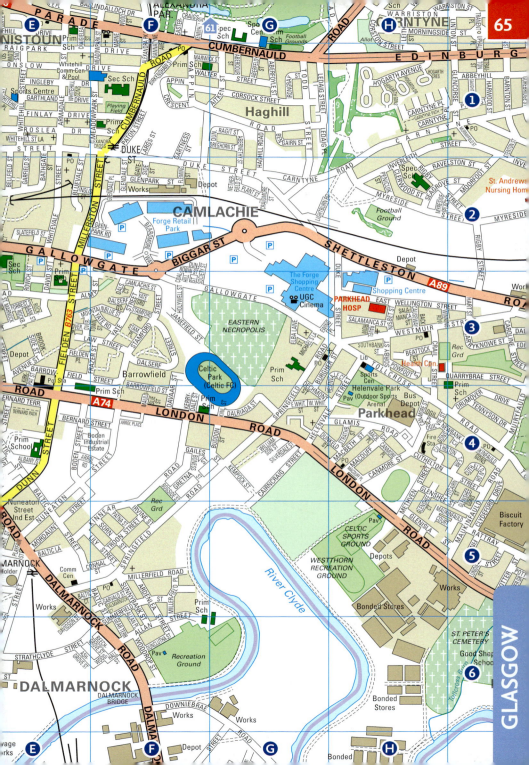

This index contains streets that are not named on the map due to insufficient space. For each of these cases the nearest street that does appear on the map is shown in *italics*.

A

Abbotsford Pl	63 H3
Abercromby Dr	64 D2
Abercromby Sq	64 D2
Abercromby St	64 D3
Aberdour St	65 G1
Aberfeldy St	65 G1
Aberfoyle St	65 G1
Abernethy St	65 G1
Academy Pk	62 C4
Acorn Ct	64 D4
Acorn St	64 D4
Adams Ct La	63 H2
Adamswell St	60 C3
Addison Rd	58 D2
Adelphi St	64 B3
Admiral St	63 E3
Aikenhead Rd	63 H5
Aird's La	
off Bridgegate	64 A2
Airlie La	58 B2
Airlie St	58 A3
Aitken St	65 G1
Albany St	65 E4
Albert Br	64 A3
Albert Cross	63 F5
Albert Dr	62 C6
Albion Gate	
off Albion St	64 B1
Albion St	64 B2
Alexander Cres	64 A4
Alexandra Ct	61 F6
Alexandra Cross	65 F1
Alexandra Par	60 C6
Alexandra Pk St	65 F1
Alford St	60 B3
Alfred La	58 D3
Alfred Ter	59 F5
Allander St	60 A2
Allan Glen Pl	60 B6
Allan Pl	65 F5
Allan St	65 F6
Allison Pl	
off Prince Edward St	63 G6
Allison St	63 G6
Alma St	65 E3
Almond St	61 H5
Alston La	
off Claythorn St	64 C2
Amisfield St	59 E1
Anchor La	
off St. Vincent Pl	64 A1
Ancroft St	59 G3
Anderson St	58 B4
Anderston Cross Cen	63 G1
Anderston Quay	63 F2
Angus St	60 C2
Annandale St	63 H5
Annbank Pl	64 D2
Annbank St	64 D2
Annette St	63 G6
Annfield Pl	64 D1
Anson St	64 D4
Anthony St	63 G1
Appin Cres	65 F1
Appin Rd	65 F1
Appleby St	59 H3
Applecross St	59 H3
Apsley La	
off Apsley St	58 A4
Apsley St	58 A4
Arcadia Pl	64 C3
Arcadia St	64 C3
Ardbeg La	63 G6
Ardbeg St	63 G6
Ardenlea St	65 F5
Ardery St	
off Apsley St	58 A4
Ardessie Pl	58 D1
Ardoch St	60 A2

Ardo Gdns	
off Hinshelwood Dr	62 A3
Argyle St	63 G1
Argyll Arc	64 A1
Ark La	64 D1
Arlington Pl	59 F5
Arlington St	59 F5
Armadale Ct	61 E6
Armadale Path	61 E6
Armadale Pl	61 E6
Armadale St	65 E1
Armour St	64 C2
Arnwood Dr	58 A1
Arrol Pl	65 F4
Arrol Rd	65 E4
Arthur St	58 D5
Ascog St	63 G6
Ashfield St	60 A2
Ashgrove St	65 E6
Ashley La	59 F5
Ashley St	59 F5
Ashton La	58 D4
Ashton La N	
off Ashton La	58 D4
Ashton Rd	58 D4
Ashvale Cres	60 C1
Aspen Dr	61 E3
Athole Gdns	58 C3
Athole La	58 C3
Atlas Ind Est	60 D2
Atlas Pl	60 D3
Atlas Rd	60 C2
Atlas Sq	
off Ayr St	60 D2
Auchentoshan Ter	60 D4
Auchinloch St	60 D3
Auckland St	59 H3
Avenuepark St	59 E2
Avenue St	65 E3
Avonspark St	61 E3
Ayr St	60 C3
Aytoun Rd	62 D5

B

Back Causeway	65 H3
Bagnell St	60 D1
Bain Sq	
off Bain St	64 C2
Bain St	64 C2
Bairds Brae	59 H3
Baird St	60 B5
Balaclava St	
off McAlpine St	63 G1
Balcarres Av	58 C1
Balgair Pl	59 H2
Balgair St	59 H1
Balglass Gdns	59 H2
Balglass St	59 H2
Balgraybank St	60 D2
Balgrayhill Rd	60 D1
Baliol La	59 F5
Baliol St	59 F5
Ballantrae Ct	63 F1
Ballater Pl	64 B4
Ballater St	64 A3
Ballindalloch Dr	61 E6
Ballindarroch La	
off Armadale St	61 E6
Balmore Sq	59 H1
Balornock Rd	61 E1
Baltic Ct	
off Baltic St	65 E5
Baltic La	65 E5
Baltic Pl	65 E4
Baltic St	65 E4
Banavie La	
off Banavie Rd	58 B3
Banavie Rd	58 A3
Bankhall St	63 H6
Bank St	59 E4
Bannatyne Av	65 F1

Barbreck Rd	
off Pollokshaws Rd	63 G6
Barclay St	
off Lenzie St	60 D1
Bardowie St	59 H2
Bargeddie St	61 H4
Barloch St	60 A2
Barmulloch Rd	61 E2
Barnhill Dr	
off Foresthall Dr	61 E3
Barrack St	64 C2
Barrington Dr	59 F4
Barrland St	63 G5
Barrowfield St	65 E3
Barr St	59 G3
Bartholomew St	65 E5
Bathgate St	65 E2
Bath La	
off Wellington St	59 G6
Bath La W	
off North St	59 F6
Bath St	59 G6
Batson St	63 H6
Beaconsfield Rd	58 B1
Beardmore Way	57 F2
Beaton Rd	63 E6
Beattock St	65 H3
Beaumont Gate	58 C3
Bedford La	63 H3
Bedford St	63 H3
Beech Av	62 B3
Beechgrove St	65 F6
Beith St	58 B5
Belgrave La	59 E3
Belgrave Ter	59 E3
Belhaven Cres La	
off Kensington Rd	58 C2
Belhaven Ter	58 C2
Belhaven Ter La	58 C2
Belhaven Ter W	58 C2
Belhaven Ter W La	58 C2
Bellevue Pl	60 D5
Bellfield St	65 E2
Bellgrove St	64 D2
Bellshaugh Ct	58 C1
Bellshaugh Gdns	58 C1
Bellshaugh La	58 C1
Bellshaugh Pl	58 C1
Bellshaugh Rd	58 C1
Bell St	64 B2
Belmont Cres	59 E3
Belmont La	59 E3
Belmont St	59 E3
Beltane St	
off Dorset St	59 F6
Benalder St	58 C5
Bengairn St	65 G1
Bennan Sq	64 A6
Benny Lynch Ct	64 A3
Benthall St	64 B4
Bentinck St	59 E5
Benview St	59 F2
Berkeley St	59 E6
Berkeley Ter La	
off Elderslie St	59 F6
Bernard Path	65 E4
Bernard St	65 E4
Bernard Ter	65 E4
Berryburn Rd	61 G2
Biggar St	65 F2
Bilsland Ct	59 H1
Bilsland Dr	59 F1
Binnie Pl	64 C3
Birchend Dr	61 F4
Birchend Pl	61 E4
Birch St	
off Silverfir St	64 B5
Birkenshaw St	65 F1
Birkwood St	
off Dalmarnock Rd	65 F6
Birnam Rd	
off London Rd	65 H5

Birnie Ct	61 G3
Birnie Rd	61 G2
Bishopmill Pl	61 G2
Bishopmill Rd	61 G1
Bishop St	63 G1
Blackburn St	62 D2
Blackie St	58 D6
Black St	60 B5
Blackthorn St	60 C1
Blairatholl Av	58 A3
Blairatholl Gdns	58 A3
Blantyre St	58 D5
Blochairn Rd	61 E5
Bluevale St	65 E2
Blythswood Ct	
off Cadogan St	63 G1
Blythswood Sq	
off Blythswood St	59 G6
Blythswood St	63 G1
Boden Ind Est	65 F4
Boden St	65 E4
Boghead Rd	61 E1
Bogside St	65 F4
Boleyn Rd	63 E6
Bonawe St	
off Kirkland St	59 F2
Boness St	65 F4
Bonhill St	59 H3
Bonnar St	65 E5
Borron St	60 A3
Botanic Cres	58 D2
Botanic Cres La	58 D2
Bothwell La	
off Blythswood St	63 G1
Bothwell St	59 G6
Boundary Rd	
off Rutherglen Rd	64 C6
Bower St	59 E3
Bowman St	63 G6
Bowmont Gdns	58 C3
Bowmont Ter	58 C3
Bradfield Av	58 C1
Braehead St	64 B5
Braemore Gdns	60 B2
Braeside St	59 F3
Braid Sq	59 G4
Braid St	59 G4
Brandon St	64 D2
Brand Pl	62 C2
Brand St	62 C2
Breadalbane St	
off St. Vincent St	59 F6
Brechin St	59 E6
Bridgegate	64 A2
Bridgegate Path	
off Bridgegate	64 A2
Bridge St	63 H2
Bridgeton Business Cen	64 D3
Bridgeton Cross	64 D3
Brighton Pl	62 B2
Brighton St	62 B2
Bright St	60 D5
Briton St	62 B2
Broadford St	60 A4
Broad St	64 D3
Brodick St	61 E5
Brookside St	65 E3
Brook St	64 D3
Broomfield La	60 D1
Broomfield Pl	60 D1
Broomfield Rd	60 D1
Broomielaw	63 G2
Broomknowes Rd	61 E2
Broomloan Ct	62 A3
Broomloan Pl	62 A2
Broomloan Rd	62 A2
Broompark Circ	60 D6
Broompark Dr	64 D1
Broompark La	64 D1

Broompark St	64 D1
Brora La	
off Brora St	61 H1
Brora St	61 H1
Brown St	63 G1
Bruce Rd	63 E5
Brunswick St	64 A1
Buccleuch La	
off Rose St	59 G6
Buccleuch St	59 G6
Buchanan St	63 H1
Buchan St	
off Norfolk St	63 H3
Buckingham St	58 D3
Buckingham Ter	58 D3
Bucksburn Rd	61 G3
Buddon St	65 G4
Bunhouse Rd	58 C5
Burgher St	65 G4
Burgh Hall La	58 B5
Burgh Hall St	58 B5
Burgh La	58 D2
Burleigh St	58 A4
Burmola St	59 H3
Burnbank Gdns	59 F4
Burnbank La	
off Napiershall St	59 F4
Burnbank Pl	
off Drygate	64 C1
Burnbank Pl (Woodside)	
off Burnbank Ter	59 G4
Burnbank Ter	59 F4
Burnbrae St	61 E3
Burndyke Ct	62 B3
Burndyke Sq	62 C2
Burndyke St	62 B3
Burns St	59 H4
Burrells La	64 C1
Bute Gdns	58 D4
Bute La	
off Great George St	58 D4
Butterbiggins Rd	63 G6
Butterfield Pl	
off Pollokshaws Rd	63 G6
Byres Rd	58 C4
Byshot St	60 B2

C

Cadogan St	63 G1
Cadzow St	63 G1
Caird Dr	58 B5
Cairncraig St	65 G4
Cairnlea Dr	62 B3
Caithness St	59 F3
Caldarvan St	59 H3
Calder St	63 H6
Caledonia Av	64 A4
Caledonian Cres	
off Great Western Rd	59 E4
Caledonia Rd	63 H4
Caledonia St	64 A4
Caledon La	58 C4
Caledon St	58 C4
Calgary St	60 A4
Callander St	59 G2
Calton Entry	
off Gallowgate	64 C2
Cambridge St	59 H6
Camden Ter	64 A4
Camlachie St	65 F2
Camp Rd	64 D4
Campsie St	60 D2
Canal St	60 A4
Candleriggs	64 B2
Canmore Pl	65 H4
Canmore St	65 H4
Canting Way	62 C2
Carberry Rd	62 D2
Carbeth St	59 H2

arbisdale St 60 C1
arbrook St 61 E5
ardarrach St 61 E1
ardow Rd 61 G2
ardross Ct 64 D1
ardross St 64 D1
ardwell St
  off Eglinton St 63 G4
ardyke St 61 E2
arfin St 63 H6
arfrae St 58 C6
arillon Rd 62 C3
arleston St 60 D2
arlisle St 60 B2
arlton Ct 63 H2
arlton Pl 63 H2
armichael St 62 B2
arnarvon St 59 F5
arnoustie Pl 63 F3
arnoustie St 63 F3
arntyne Path 65 H1
arntyne Pl 65 H1
arntyne Rd 65 G2
arrick St 63 G2
arrington St 59 F4
arron Cres 60 B3
arron Pl 60 B3
arron St 60 C1
arstairs St 65 E6
astlebank Cres 58 A5
astle Cres N Ct
  off Royal Ex Sq 64 A1
astle St 60 C6
astle St (Partick) 58 C5
athedral Sq 64 C1
athedral St 60 A6
atherine Pl
  off Hydepark St 63 F1
avendish Ct 63 H4
avendish Pl 63 H4
avendish St 63 H4
ecil St 58 D3
edar Ct 59 G4
edar St 59 G4
entral Sta 63 H1
entre St 63 G3
essnock St 62 C2
halmers Ct 64 C2
halmers Gate
halmers Pl
  off Claythorn St 64 C2
halmers St
  off Claythorn St 64 C2
heapside St 63 F2
helmsford Dr 58 B1
hesterfield Av 58 A1
hestnut St
hisholm St 64 B2
hristopher St 61 E4
hurchill Dr 58 A3
hapman St
  off Allison St 63 G6
haring Cross 59 F5
haring Cross La
  off Granville St 59 F6
harles St 60 C5
harlotte La
  off London Rd 64 B2
harlotte La S
  off Charlotte St 64 B2
harlotte La W
  off London Rd 64 B2
harlotte St 64 B2

Claremont St 59 E6
Claremont Ter 59 F5
Claremont Ter La 59 E5
Clarence Dr 58 A3
Clarence Gdns 58 A3
Clarence La 58 B3
Clarendon La
  off Clarendon St 59 G4
Clarendon Pl 59 G4
Clarendon St 59 G4
Clare St 61 E4
Clayslaps Rd 58 D5
Claythorn Av 64 C3
Claythorn Circ
  off Claythorn Av 64 C2
Claythorn Ct
  off Claythorn Pk 64 C2
Claythorn Pk 64 C3
Claythorn St 64 C2
Claythorn Ter
  off Claythorn Pk 64 C2
Clayton Ter 64 D1
Cleghorn St 59 H3
Cleland La 64 A3
Cleland St 64 A3
Clerwood St 65 H2
Cleveden Cres 58 B1
Cleveden Cres La 58 B1
Cleveden Dr 58 B1
Cleveden Dr La
  off Mirrlees Dr 58 C2
Cleveden Gdns 58 C1
Cleveland La
  off Kent Rd 58 D5
Cleveland St 59 F6
Clifford Gdns 62 B3
Clifford La
Clifford Pl
  off Clifford St 62 D2
Clifford St 62 B3
Cliff Rd 59 F5
Clifton Pl
  off Clifton St 59 E5
Clifton St 59 E5
Closeburn St 60 A1
Clouston Ct
  off Fergus Dr 59 E2
Clouston La 59 E2
Clouston St 58 D2
Cloverbank Gdns 61 E5
Cloverbank St 61 E5
Clutha St
  off Paisley Rd W 62 D2
Clydebrae St 58 B6
Clyde Ind Cen 59 E6
Clyde Pl 63 G2
Clydeside
  Expressway 58 C6
Clydeside Rd 64 D6
Clyde St 63 H2
Clynder St 62 B2
Coalhill St 65 F3
Cobden Rd 60 D4
Coburg St 63 H3
Cochrane St 64 A1
Cockmuir St 61 E2
Colbert St 64 D5
Coldstream Pl 60 A3
Colebrooke La
  off Colebrooke St 59 E3
Colebrooke Pl 59 E3
Colebrooke St 59 E3
Colebrooke Ter 59 E3
College St 64 B1
Collins St 64 C1
Coll Pl 61 F4
Coll St 61 E4
Columba St 62 B1
Colvend La 64 D5
Colvend St 64 D5
Comelypark Pl
  off Comelypark St 65 E2
Comelypark St 64 D2
Commerce St 63 H3
Commercial Ct 64 B3
Commercial Rd 64 A4

Congress Rd 62 D1
Congress Way 63 E1
Connal St 65 F5
Contin Pl 58 D1
Cook St 63 G3
Cooperage Pl 58 C6
Coopers Well La
  off Dumbarton Rd 58 C5
Coopers Well St 58 C5
Copland Pl 62 B1
Copland Quad 62 B2
Copland Rd 62 B2
Coplaw Ct 63 G5
Coplaw St 63 G5
Cornhill St 61 E1
Corn St 59 H4
Cornwall St 62 D3
Cornwall St S 62 D4
Corsock St 65 G1
Corston St 61 H6
Corunna St 59 E6
Cotton St 64 D6
Coulin Gdns 60 B2
Couper Pl 60 B5
Couper St 60 B5
Coventry Dr 61 F6
Cowan La 59 E4
Cowan St 59 E4
Cowcaddens Rd 59 H5
Cowcaddens St
  off Renfield St 59 H5
Cowlairs Rd 60 C2
Coxhill St 60 B3
Craigenbay St 61 F2
Craigendmuir St 61 H4
Craighall Rd 59 H4
Craighead Av 61 H3
Craigiehall Pl 62 D2
Craigiehall St
  off Craigiehall Pl 62 D2
Craigielea St 61 E6
Craigie St 63 G6
Craigmaddie Ter La
  off Derby St 59 E5
Craigmont Dr 59 E1
Craigmore St 65 G2
Craignethan Gdns
  off Lawrie St 58 B4
Craigpark 65 E1
Craigpark Dr 65 E1
Craigpark Ter
  off Craigpark 65 E1
Crail St 65 H3
Cramond St 64 B6
Cranborne Rd 58 A1
Cranston St 59 F6
Cranworth La 58 D3
Cranworth St 58 D3
Crathie Dr 58 A4
Crathie La
  off Exeter Dr 58 A4
Crawford La
  off Crawford St 58 A4
Crawford Path
  off Crawford St 58 A4
Crawford St 58 A4
Cresswell La 58 D3
Cresswell St 58 D3
Crichton Pl
  off Crichton St 60 C2
Crichton St 60 C2
Crieff Ct
  off North St 59 F6
Crimea St 63 G1
Crinan St 61 F6
Croftbank St 60 D2
Cromer Gdns 59 F1
Cromwell La 59 G4
Cromwell St 59 G4
Crown Circ 58 C3
Crown Ct
  off Virginia St 64 A1
Crown Gdns 58 C3
Crown Mans
  *off North Gardner
  St* 58 B3

Crownpoint Rd 64 D3
Crown Rd N 58 B3
Crown Rd S 58 B3
Crown St 64 A3
Crown Ter 58 B3
Crow Rd 58 A3
Croy Pl 61 G1
Croy Rd 61 G1
Cubie St 64 D3
Culloden St 61 F6
Cumberland Pl 64 A4
Cumberland St 63 H3
Cumbernauld Rd 65 F1
Custom Ho Quay
  off Clyde St 64 A2
Cuthbertson St 63 G6
Cuthelton St 65 H4
Cuthelton Ter 65 H4
Cypress St 60 B1

D
Dalcross La
  off Byres Rd 58 C4
Dalcross Pas
  off Dalcross St 58 C4
Dalcross St 58 C4
Dale Path 64 D4
Dale St 64 D4
Dalhousie La
  off Dalhousie St 59 G5
Dalhousie St 59 G5
Dalintober St 63 G3
Dalkeith Av 62 B4
Dalmally St 59 F3
Dalmarnock Br 65 F6
Dalmarnock Ct 65 F5
Dalmarnock Dr 64 D4
Dalmarnock Rd 64 D4
Dalmeny St 64 C6
Dalnair St 58 C5
Dalriada St 65 G4
Dalserf Ct 65 F3
Dalserf Gdns 65 F3
Dalserf St 65 F3
Dalziel Dr 62 C5
Dalziel Quad 62 C5
Dargarvel Av 62 B4
Dargarvel Path
  off Dumbreck Av 62 A5
Darnick St 61 F3
Darnley Gdns 63 E6
Darnley Pl
  off Darnley Rd 63 E6
Darnley Rd 63 E6
Darnley St 63 F6
Dartford St 59 H3
Davaar St 65 F4
Dava St 62 A1
Davidson St 65 E6
David St 65 E3
Dawson Pl 59 H3
Dawson Rd 59 H3
Deanside La
  off Rottenrow 64 B1
Dechmont St 65 G3
Dee St 61 H5
Denham St 59 H3
Denmark St 60 A2
Derby St 59 E6
Derby Ter La 59 E5
Derwent St 59 H2
Deveron St 61 H5
Devon Pl 63 H4
Devonshire Gdns 58 B2
Devonshire Gdns La
  off Hyndland Rd 58 B2
Devonshire Ter 58 B2
Devonshire Ter La 58 B2
Devon St 63 H4
Dick St 59 F3
Dinart St 61 H5
Dinwiddie St 61 G4
Dixons Blazes
  Ind Est 64 A5
Dixon St 63 H2
Dobbies Ln 59 H5

Dobbies Ln Pl 60 B6
Dolphin Rd 62 D6
Doncaster St 59 G2
Don St 61 H6
Dora St 64 D5
Dornoch St 64 D3
Dorset Sq
  off Dorset St 59 F6
Dorset St 59 F6
Douglas La
  *off West Regent
  St* 59 G6
Douglas St 59 G6
Douglas Ter
  off Glencairn Dr 63 F5
Doune Gdns 59 E3
Doune Gdns La 59 E3
Doune Quad 59 E3
Dover St 59 E6
Dowanhill St 58 C3
Dowanside La
  off Byres Rd 58 D3
Dowanside Rd 58 C3
Downiebrae Rd 65 F6
Downs St 60 D2
Drake St 64 C3
Dreghorn St 65 G1
Drem Pl
  off Merkland St 58 B4
Drumbottie Rd 61 E1
Drumpellier St 61 H4
Drury St
  off Renfield St 63 H1
Dryburgh Gdns
  off Wilton St 59 F3
Drygate 64 C1
Duchray La 61 H5
Duchray St 61 H5
Dudley Dr 58 A3
Dudley La 58 A3
Duke St 64 C1
Dumbarton Rd 58 A4
Dumbreck Av 62 A4
Dumbreck Ct 62 A5
Dumbreck Path
  off Dumbreck Av 62 A4
Dumbreck Pl 62 A5
Dumbreck Rd 62 B5
Dumbreck Sq 62 A4
Dunard St 59 F2
Dunaskin St 58 C5
Dunbeith Pl 58 D1
Dunblane St 59 H5
Dunchattan Pl 64 D1
Dunchattan St 64 D1
Dunclutha St 65 F6
Dundashill 59 H4
Dundas La 60 A6
Dundas St 60 A6
Dundasvale Ct
  off Maitland St 59 H5
Dundasvale Rd
  off Maitland St 59 H5
Dundonald Rd 58 C2
Dunearn St 59 F4
Dunkeld St 65 G4
Dunlop St 64 A2
Dunmore La
  off Norfolk St 63 H3
Dunn St 65 E4
Dunolly St 61 E5
Dunragit St 65 G1
Dunrobin St 65 F2
Dunsmuir St 62 B1
Duntroon St 61 F6
Durham St 62 D3
Dyce La 58 A4
Dykemuir Pl
  off Dykemuir St 61 F2
Dykemuir Quad
  off Dykemuir St 61 E2
Dykemuir St 61 E2

E
Eaglesham Ct
  off Blackburn St 63 E2

Eaglesham Pl	63	E2
Eagle St	60	A4
Earlston Av	60	D5
Earlston Pl	60	C5
Earnock St	61	H2
East Bath La		
off Sauchiehall St	60	A6
Eastburn Rd	61	F1
East Campbell St	64	C2
Eastcroft Ter	61	E2
Eastercraigs	61	F6
Eastfield Rd	59	G3
Eastvale Pl	58	C6
East Wellington		
St	65	H3
East Whitby St	65	G4
Eccles St		
off Carron St	60	C1
Edelweiss Ter		
off Gardner St	58	B4
Eden La	61	H5
Eden St	61	H5
Edgefauld Av	60	D3
Edgefauld Dr	60	D2
Edgefauld Pl	60	D1
Edgefauld Rd	60	D2
Edgehill La	58	A2
Edinburgh Rd	65	H1
Edington St	59	H4
Edwin St	62	D3
Eglinton Ct	63	H3
Eglinton St	63	H3
Elba La		
off Gallowgate	65	G3
Elcho St	64	D2
Elderslie St	59	F5
Eldon Ct		
off Caird Dr	58	B4
Eldon St	59	E4
Elgin St		
off Rowchester St	65	E3
Elie St	58	C4
Elizabeth St	62	C3
Ellesmere St	59	G2
Elliot Pl		
off Finnieston St	59	E6
Elliot St	63	E1
Elmbank Cres	59	G6
Elmbank La		
off North St	59	F6
Elmbank St	59	G6
Elmbank St La	59	G6
Elmfoot St	64	B6
Elmvale Row	60	C1
Elmvale Row E		
off Elmvale Row	60	C1
Elmvale Row W		
off Elmvale Row	60	C1
Elmvale St	60	C1
Elphinstone Pl	62	C1
Eltham St		
off Bonhill St	59	H3
Endrick St	60	B3
Errol Gdns	64	A4
Erskine Av	62	B4
Esmond St	58	C5
Eton La	59	E4
Ewing Pl	65	G3
Exchange Pl		
off Buchanan St	64	A1
Exeter Dr	58	A4
Exeter La		
off Exeter Dr	58	A4

F

Fairbairn Path		
off Ruby St	65	E4
Fairbairn St	65	E4
Fairley St	62	B2
Fairlie Pk Dr	58	A4
Falfield St	63	G4
Falkland La	58	B3
Falkland St	58	B3
Farm Rd	62	B3
Farnell St	59	H4
Fauldhouse St	64	B5

Fergus Ct		
off Fergus Dr	59	E2
Fergus Dr	59	E2
Fergus La	59	F2
Fernbank St	60	C1
Ferry Rd	58	B5
Fielden Pl	65	E3
Fielden St	65	E3
Findhorn St	61	H6
Finlas St	60	B2
Finlay Dr	61	E1
Finnart Sq	64	D5
Finnart St	64	D5
Finnieston Quay	63	E1
Finnieston Sq		
off Finnieston St	59	E6
Finnieston St	63	E1
Firhill Rd	59	G2
Firhill St	59	G2
Firpark Pl		
off Firpark St	60	D6
Firpark St	60	D6
Firpark Ter	64	D1
First Gdns	62	A4
Fisher Ct	64	D1
Fitzroy La	59	E6
Fitzroy Pl		
off Royal Ter	59	E5
Fleming St	65	F2
Flemington St	60	D3
Fleurs Av	62	B4
Fleurs Rd	62	B4
Florence St	64	A3
Forbes Dr	64	D3
Forbes St	64	D2
Fordneuk St	65	E3
Ford Rd	58	D2
Fordyce St	58	B4
Foremount		
Ter La	58	B3
Foresthall Cres	61	E3
Foresthall Dr	61	E3
Forge Pl	61	F4
Forge Retail Pk	65	F2
Forge Shop Cen,		
The	65	G3
Forge St	61	F4
Forrestfield St	61	E5
Forrest St	65	E3
Forth St	63	F5
Fortrose St	58	B4
Fotheringay La	62	D6
Fotheringay Rd	62	D6
Foundry St	60	D2
Fountainwell Av	60	B3
Fountainwell Dr	60	B4
Fountainwell Pl	60	B4
Fountainwell Rd	60	B4
Fountainwell Sq	60	C4
Fountainwell Ter	60	C4
Fourth Gdns	62	A4
Fox St	63	H2
Foyers Ter	61	E2
Francis St	63	G4
Frankfield St	61	H4
Franklin St	64	D5
Frazer St	65	E3
French St	64	D5
Fruin Pl	60	A2
Fruin St	60	A2

G

Gadie St	61	H6
Gadshill St	60	D5
Gailes St	65	F4
Gallowgate	64	B2
Gardner St	58	B4
Garfield St	65	E2
Garmouth Ct	58	A6
Garnet Ct		
off New City Rd	59	G5
Garnethill St	59	G5
Garnet St	59	G5
Garnock St	60	D4
Garrioch Cres	58	D1
Garrioch Dr	58	D1

Garrioch Gate		
off Garrioch Rd	59	E1
Garriochmill Rd	59	E2
Garriochmill Way		
off South		
Woodside Rd	59	F3
Garrioch Quad	58	D1
Garrioch Rd	58	D2
Garscube Cross	59	H4
Garscube Rd	59	G3
Gartferry St	60	D2
Garthland Dr	65	E1
Garth St		
off Glassford St	64	A1
Gartness St	65	F1
Gartons Rd	61	G1
Garvald Ct		
off Baltic St	65	E6
Garvald St	65	F5
Gateside St	65	F2
Gear Ter	65	F6
General Terminus		
Quay	63	F2
George Sq	64	A1
George St	64	A1
Gibson St		
(Calton)	64	C2
Gibson St		
(Hillhead)	59	E4
Gilbert St	58	C6
Gilmour Pl	64	A4
Girvan St	61	H5
Gladstone St	59	G4
Glamis Rd	65	H4
Glasgow Br	63	H2
Glasgow Cross	64	B2
Glasgow Grn	64	B3
Glasgow Rd	64	D6
Glasgow St	59	E3
Glassford St	64	A1
Glebe Ct	60	B6
Glebe St	60	B5
Glenapp St	63	F5
Glenbarr St	60	D5
Glencairn Dr	62	D6
Glencairn Gdns	63	E6
Glencairn La	63	F6
Glendale Pl	65	F2
Glendale St	65	F2
Glendarvel Gdns	60	B2
Glenfarg St	59	G4
Glenisla St	65	H5
Glenmavis St	59	H5
Glenpark Rd	65	F2
Glenpark St	65	F2
Glenshee Ct	65	H5
Glenshee St	65	H4
Glentrool Gdns	60	A2
Gloucester St	63	G3
Golfhill Dr	61	E6
Golfhill Ter		
off Firpark St	60	D6
Golspie St	58	A6
Goosedubbs		
off Stockwell St	64	A2
Gorbals Cross	64	A3
Gorbals La		
off Oxford St	63	H2
Gorbals St	63	H4
Gordon La		
off Mitchell St	63	H1
Gordon St	63	H1
Gorstan Pl		
off Wyndford Rd	58	C1
Gough St	61	H6
Gourlay Path		
off Endrick St	60	B3
Gourlay St	60	B3
Gourock St		
off Eglinton St	63	G4
Govan Cross		
off Govan Rd	58	A6
Govan Cross Shop		
Cen	58	A6
Govanhill St	63	H6
Govan Rd	62	C2

Gower La		
off North Gower		
St	62	D3
Gower St	62	C4
Gower Ter	62	C3
Grace St	63	F1
Grafton Pl	60	A6
Graham Sq	64	D2
Graignestock Pl		
off London Rd	64	C3
Graignestock St	64	C3
Granby La	58	D3
Granton St	64	C6
Grant St	59	F5
Granville St	59	F6
Gray St	59	E5
Great Dovehill	64	B2
Great George St	58	D3
Great Kelvin La		
off Glasgow St	59	E4
Great Western Rd	59	E3
Great Western		
Ter	58	C2
Great Western		
Ter La	58	C2
Green, The	64	C3
Greendyke St	64	B2
Greenhead St	64	C4
Greenlodge Ter		
off Greenhead St	64	C4
Greenrig St	61	H3
Green St	64	C3
Gretna St	65	F4
Grier Path		
off Crail St	65	H3
Grierson La		
off Lomax St	61	H6
Grierson St	61	H6
Grosvenor Cres	58	D3
Grosvenor Cres La		
off Byres Rd	58	D3
Grosvenor La	58	D3
Grosvenor Ter	58	D3
Grovepark Ct	59	G4
Grovepark Gdns	59	G4
Grovepark Pl	59	G3
Grovepark St	59	G3
Gullane St	58	B5

H

Haggswood Av	62	C6
Haghill Rd	65	G2
Haig St	60	D2
Hallside Pl	64	A4
Hamilton Av	62	D5
Hamilton Dr	59	E3
Hamiltonhill Cres		
off Hamiltonhill		
Rd	59	H2
Hamiltonhill Rd	59	H3
Hamilton Pk Av	59	E3
Handel Pl	64	A4
Hannover Ct	60	A6
Hanover St	64	A1
Hanson Pk	60	D6
Hanson St	60	D6
Harcourt Dr	61	F6
Harley St	62	C3
Harmony Ct	62	A1
Harmony Pl	62	A1
Harmony Row	62	A1
Harmony Sq		
off Harmony		
Row	62	A1
Harrison Dr		
off Copland Rd	62	B2
Harvey St	60	A4
Harvie St	62	D2
Hastie St	58	D5
Hathaway La	59	E1
Hathaway St	59	E1
Haugh Rd	58	D6
Havelock La	58	C4
Havelock St	58	C4
Hawthorn Quad	60	A1
Hawthorn St	60	A1

Hayburn Ct		
off Hayburn St	58	B5
Hayburn Cres	58	A5
Hayburn Gate	58	A5
Hayburn La	58	A5
Hayburn Pl		
off Hayburn St	58	B5
Hayburn St	58	B5
Hayfield Ct	64	B4
Hayfield St	64	B4
Hayston Cres	59	H1
Hayston St	59	H1
Hazelwood Rd	62	C5
Heddle Pl		
off Cadogan St	63	G1
Helen St	62	A2
Helenvale Ct	65	H3
Helenvale St	65	H3
Henderson St	59	F1
Herbertson St	63	H3
Herbert St	59	F3
Heron St	64	D5
Herries Rd	62	C6
Herriet St	63	F6
Hickman Ter	64	A6
Hickory St	60	C1
Highburgh Rd	58	C3
High Craighall		
Rd	59	H4
Highland La	58	C6
High St	64	B1
Hillfoot St	65	E1
Hillhead Pl		
off Bank St	59	E4
Hillhead St	58	D4
Hillhouse St	61	E3
Hillkirk Pl		
off Hillkirk St	60	C3
Hillkirk St	60	C3
Hillkirk St La		
off Hillkirk St	60	D3
Hillsborough Ter		
off Bower St	59	E4
Hillside Gdns La		
off North		
Gardner St	58	B3
Hill St	59	G5
Hinshaw St	59	G4
Hinshelwood Dr	62	A2
Hobart St	59	H5
Hobden St	61	E4
Hogarth Av	65	H2
Hogarth Cres	65	H2
Hogarth Dr	65	H2
Hogarth Gdns	65	H2
Hoganfield Ct	61	H4
Hoganfield St	61	H4
Holland St	59	G6
Hollybank St	61	E5
Hollybrook Pl		
off Hollybrook St	64	A6
Hollybrook St	64	A6
Holly Dr	61	E2
Holm St	63	G1
Holyrood Cres	59	F4
Holyrood Quad	59	F4
Holywell St	65	F3
Hopefield Av	58	C2
Hopehill Gdns	59	H4
Hopehill Rd	59	G4
Hope St	63	H1
Hopetoun Ter	61	E2
Horne St		
off Hawthorn St	60	C1
Hornshill St	61	E2
Horselethill Rd	58	C3
Hospital St	64	A4
Hotspur St	59	E1
Houldsworth La		
off Finnieston St	59	E6
Houldsworth St	59	E6
Houston Pl	63	F1
Houston St	63	F1
Howard St	63	H2
Howat St	58	A6
Hughenden Dr	58	B2

Name	Grid
ughenden Gdns	58 A2
ughenden La	58 B2
ughenden Rd	58 B2
ughenden Ter	58 B2
off Hughenden Rd	58 B2
ugo St	59 F1
unter St	64 C2
untingdon Rd	60 C4
untingdon Sq	60 C4
untly Gdns	58 C3
untly Rd	58 C3
utcheson St	64 A1
utchinsontown Ct	64 A4
ydepark St	63 F1
yndland Av	58 B4
yndland Rd	58 B2
yndland St	58 C4
maica St	63 H2
ames Morrison St	
off St. Andrews Sq	64 B2
ames Nisbet St	60 C6
ames St	64 C4
ames Watt La	
off James Watt St	63 G1
ames Watt St	63 G1
amieson Ct	63 H6
amieson Path	
off Jamieson St	63 H6
amieson St	63 H6
anefield St	65 F3
ane Pl	64 A4
ardine St	
off Tillie St	59 F3
edburgh Gdns	
off Wilton St	59 F3
essie St	64 B6
ocelyn Sq	64 A2
ohn Knox La	
off Drygate	64 C1
ohn Knox St	64 C1
ohn St	64 A1
ulian Av	58 C2
ulian La	58 C2

K

Name	Grid
arol Path	
off St. Peters St	59 G4
ay St	60 D2
eir St	63 F5
eith Ct	58 C5
eith St	58 C4
elbourne St	59 E2
ellas St	62 A1
elty Pl	
off Bedford St	63 H3
elvin Dr	58 D2
elvingrove St	59 E6
elvinhaugh Gate	58 D6
elvinhaugh Pl	
off Kelvingrove St	58 D6
elvinhaugh St	58 C6

Name	Grid
Kelvinside Av	59 E2
Kelvinside Dr	59 F2
Kelvinside Gdns	59 E2
Kelvinside Gdns E	59 F3
Kelvinside Gdns La	59 E2
Kelvinside Ter S	59 E2
Kelvinside Ter W	59 E3
Kelvin Way	58 D5
Kempock St	65 G4
Kemp St	60 C2
Kennedy Path	
off St. Mungo Pl	60 B6
Kennedy St	60 B5
Kennet St	61 E5
Kennyhill Sq	61 F6
Kensington Gate	
off Kensington Rd	58 C2
Kensington Gate La	58 C2
Kensington Rd	58 C2
Kent Rd	59 E6
Kent St	64 C2
Keppochhill Dr	60 B3
Keppochhill Pl	60 B4
Keppochhill Rd	60 A3
Keppochhill Way	60 B4
Keppoch St	60 B3
Kerr Dr	64 D3
Kerr Pl	64 D3
Kerr St	64 D3
Kerrydale St	65 F4
Kersland La	58 D3
Kersland St	58 D3
Kessock Dr	59 H3
Kessock Pl	59 H3
Kew Gdns	
off Ruthven St	58 D3
Kew La	58 D3
Kew Ter	58 D3
Kidston Pl	64 A4
Kidston Ter	64 A4
Kilbarchan St	
off Bedford St	63 H3
Kilberry St	61 E5
Kilbirnie Pl	63 G4
Kilbirnie St	63 G4
Kilbride St	64 B6
Kildonan Dr	58 A4
Kildrostan St	63 F6
Killearn St	59 H2
Killermont St	60 A6
Killiegrew Rd	62 D6
Kilmair Pl	58 D1
Kinbuck St	60 B2
Kingarth La	63 G6
Kingarth St	63 G6
King George V Br	63 H2
Kingsborough Gdns	58 B3
Kingsborough Gate	
off Prince Albert Rd	58 B3
Kingsborough La	58 B3
Kingsborough La E	58 B3
King's Br	64 B4
Kings Cross	64 D1
King's Dr	64 C4
Kingston Br	63 G2
Kingston Ind Est	63 F3
Kingston St	63 G2
King St	64 A2
Kinloch St	65 G4
Kinnear Rd	65 F5
Kinning Pk Ind Est	63 F3
Kinning St	63 G3
Kinnoul La	
off Downanside Rd	58 C3
Kintra St	62 B1
Kintyre St	61 E5
Kirkcaldy Rd	62 D6
Kirkhill Dr	59 E1

Name	Grid
Kirkhill Pl	58 D1
off Kirkhill Dr	58 D1
Kirkland St	59 F3
Kirklee Circ	58 C2
Kirklee Gdns	58 C1
Kirklee Gdns La	58 D2
Kirklee Gate	58 D2
Kirklee Pl	58 D2
Kirklee Quad	58 D2
Kirklee Quad La	
off Kirklee Quad	58 D2
Kirklee Rd	58 C2
Kirklee Ter	58 C2
Kirklee Ter La	58 C2
Kirkmichael Av	
off Blairatholl Av	58 A3
Kirkmichael Gdns	
off Blairatholl Av	58 A3
Kirkpatrick St	65 E3
Kirkwood St	62 C3
Knowehead Gdns	63 E5
Knowehead Ter	63 E5
Kyle St	60 A5

L

Name	Grid
La Belle Allee	59 E5
La Belle Pl	59 E5
Laburnum Rd	62 C4
La Crosse Ter	59 E3
Ladywell St	64 C1
Laidlaw St	63 G3
Laird Pl	64 D4
Lambhill Quad	63 E3
Lambhill St	62 D3
Lanark St	64 B2
Lancaster Cres	58 C2
Lancaster Cres La	58 C2
Lancaster Ter	58 C2
Lancaster Ter La	
off Westbourne Gdns W	58 B3
Lancefield Quay	63 E1
Lancefield St	63 F1
Landressy Pl	64 C4
Landressy St	64 D4
Lane Gdns	
off North Gardner St	58 B3
Langbank St	
off Eglinton St	63 H3
Langrig Rd	61 E2
Langshot St	62 D3
Lansdowne Cres	59 F4
Lansdowne Cres La	59 F4
Larbert St	59 H5
Larch Rd	62 B3
Largs St	65 F1
Latherton Dr	58 D1
Latherton Pl	
off Latherton Dr	58 D1
Laudedale La	58 B3
Lauderdale Gdns	58 B3
Laurel Pl	58 A3
Laurel St	58 A4
Laurieston Rd	63 H4
Laverockhall St	60 D3
Lawmoor Av	64 A5
Lawmoor Pl	64 A6
Lawmoor Rd	64 A5
Lawmoor St	64 A5
Lawrence St	58 C4
Lawrie St	58 B4
Law St	65 E3
Leadburn Rd	61 G2
Leader St	61 H5
Ledaig Pl	65 G1
Ledaig St	65 G1
Leicester Av	58 B1
Leith St	61 H6
Lendel Pl	
off Paisley Rd W	62 D3
Leny St	59 F2
Lenzie St	60 D1

Name	Grid
Lenzie Ter	60 D1
Leslie Rd	63 E5
Leslie St	63 F5
Lettoch St	62 A1
Leven St	63 F5
Leyden Ct	59 E1
Leyden Gdns	59 E1
Leyden St	59 E1
Liberton St	61 H6
Lightburn Rd	65 G2
Lilybank Gdns	58 D4
Lilybank Gdns La	58 D4
Lilybank La	
off Lilybank Gdns	58 D4
Lilybank Ter	
off Great George St	58 D4
Lily St	65 F5
Lincluden Path	
off McCulloch St	63 F4
Linfern Rd	58 C3
Lismore Rd	58 B1
Lister St	60 B5
Little Dovehill	
off Gallowgate	64 B2
Little St	
off McIntyre St	63 F1
Lloyd St	61 E6
Lochgreen St	61 H3
Lochsloy Ct	60 B2
Lockhart St	61 F4
Logan St	64 B5
Lomax St	61 H6
Lomond St	59 H1
London Arc	
off London Rd	64 B2
London La	
off London Rd	64 B2
London Rd	64 B2
London Way	64 B2
Longford St	61 H6
Lorne St	62 D2
Lorraine Gdns	
off Kensington Rd	58 C2
Lorraine Gdns La	
off Westbourne Gdns La	58 C2
Lorraine Rd	
off Kensington Rd	58 C2
Lossie St	61 H5
Lothian Gdns	
off Wilton St	59 E3
Loudon Ter	
off Observatory Rd	58 D3
Lovat St	
off Borron St	60 A4
Lowther Ter	
off Redlands La	58 C2
Luath St	58 A6
Lumloch St	61 E2
Lumsden St	58 D6
Lymburn St	58 D5
Lyndhurst Gdns	59 F3
Lyndhurst Gdns La	59 E2
Lynedoch Cres	59 F5
Lynedoch Cres La	59 F5
Lynedoch Pl	59 F5
Lynedoch St	59 F5
Lynedoch Ter	59 F5

M

Name	Grid
McAlpine St	63 G1
McAslin Ct	60 B6
McAslin St	60 C6
Macbeth Pl	65 H4
Macbeth St	65 H4
McCulloch St	63 F4
Macduff Pl	65 H4
Macduff St	65 H4
McFarlane St	64 C2
McIntosh Ct	64 D1
McIntosh St	64 D1
McIntyre St	63 F1

Name	Grid
McKechnie St	58 A6
Mackeith St	64 D4
Mackie St	
off Borron St	60 A4
Mackinlay St	63 H4
Maclean Sq	62 D2
Maclean St	62 D2
Maclellan St	62 C3
Macleod St	60 C6
McNeil Gdns	64 B4
McNeil St	64 B4
McPhail St	64 C4
McPhater St	59 H5
Madras Pl	64 D5
Madras St	64 D5
Mafeking St	62 B2
Main St	64 D5
Mair St	63 E2
Maitland St	59 H5
Malloch St	59 E1
Malta Ter	63 H4
Maltbarns St	59 G3
Malvern Ct	65 E2
Manresa Pl	59 H4
Mansel St	60 D1
Mansfield St	58 C4
Mansion St	60 A1
Maple Rd	62 B4
March La	
off Nithsdale Dr	63 F6
Marchmont Ter	
off Observatory Rd	58 C3
March St	63 F6
Marine Cres	63 E2
Marine Gdns	
off Mavisbank Gdns	63 F2
Mariscat Rd	63 E6
Marlow St	63 E4
Marne St	65 F1
Martha St	60 A6
Martin St	64 D5
Mart St	
off Bridgegate	64 A2
Marwick St	65 F1
Maryhill Rd	59 F3
Maryhill Shop Cen	59 E1
Maryston Pl	61 H4
Maryston St	61 H4
Mary St	59 H4
Marywood Sq	63 F6
Masterton St	60 A3
Matilda Rd	63 E4
Mauchline St	63 G4
Maukinfauld Ct	65 H5
Mauldslie St	65 F4
Maule Dr	58 A4
Mavisbank Gdns	63 E2
Maxwell Av	63 E4
Maxwell Ct	
off St. John's Rd	63 E4
Maxwell Dr	62 C4
Maxwell Gdns	62 D4
Maxwell Gro	62 D4
Maxwell La	
off Maxwell Dr	63 E4
Maxwell Oval	63 F4
Maxwell Pl	63 G5
Maxwell Rd	63 F4
Maxwell St	64 A2
Maxwell Ter	63 E4
Maxwelton Rd	61 H4
Meadowpark St	65 F1
Meadow Rd	58 A4
Meadowside St	58 A5
Megan Gate	
off Megan St	64 D4
Megan St	64 D4
Melbourne St	64 D2
Meldrum Gdns	62 D6
Melfort Av	62 B4
Melrose Gdns	59 F3
Melrose St	
off Queens Cres	59 F4
Melvaig Pl	58 D1

Melville Ct
off Brunswick St 64 B2
Melville St 63 F5
Memel St 60 C1
Menzies Dr 61 E1
Menzies Pl 61 E1
Menzies Rd 61 E1
Merchant La 64 A2
Merkland Ct
off Vine St 58 B5
Merkland St 58 B4
Merrick Gdns 62 B3
Merrick Path
off Merrick Gdns 62 B3
Merryland Pl 62 B1
Merryland St 62 B1
Methven St 65 H5
Metropole La
off Clyde St 64 A2
Middlesex Gdns 63 E2
Middlesex St 63 E3
Middleton St 62 C2
Midland St 63 H1
Midlock St 62 C3
Midton St 60 D3
Midwharf St 60 A4
Migvie Pl
off Wyndford Rd 58 D1
Milan St 63 G5
Millarbank St 60 C2
Millburn St 60 D5
Mill Cres 64 D5
Millcroft Rd 64 D6
Millerfield Pl 65 F5
Millerfield Rd 65 F5
Millerston St 65 E2
Miller St 64 A1
Millroad Dr 64 C2
Millroad Gdns 64 D2
Millroad St 64 C2
Mill St 64 D5
Milnbank St 61 E6
Milnpark Gdns 62 D3
Milnpark St 63 E3
Milton St 60 A5
Minerva St 59 E6
Minerva Way 59 E6
Mingarry La
off Clouston St 59 E2
Mingarry St 59 E2
Mireton St 59 H1
Mirrlees Dr 58 C2
Mirrlees La 58 C2
Mitchell La 63 H1
Mitchell St 63 H1
Moffat St 64 B4
Moir St 64 B2
Molendinar Gdns 61 H4
Molendinar St 64 B2
Mollinsburn St 60 C3
Monar Dr
off Monar St 59 H3
Monar Pl
off Monar St 59 H3
Monar St 59 H3
Monart Pl 59 F1
Moncur St 64 C2
Monkscroft Av 58 A3
Monkscroft Ct
off Crow Rd 58 A4
Monkscroft Gdns
off Monkscroft Av 58 A3
Montague La 58 B2
Montague St 59 F4
Monteith Pl 64 C3
Monteith Row 64 C3
Monteith Row La
off Monteith Pl 64 C3
Montgomery St 65 E4
Montrose St 60 B6
Moodiesburn St 61 H4
Moore St
off Gallowgate 64 D2
Moray Pl 63 E6
Mordaunt St 65 E5
Morgan Ms 63 H5

Morningside St 61 H6
Morrin Path
off Crichton St 60 C2
Morrin Sq
off Collins St 60 C6
Morrin St 60 C2
Morrison Ct 63 H1
Morrison St 63 G2
Mosesfield St 60 D1
Mosque Av 64 A3
Mountainblue St 65 E3
Mount St 59 F3
Moy St
off Church St 58 C4
Muirhead St
off Purdon St 58 B4
Muirpark St 58 B4
Mull St 61 F4
Murano St 59 F2
Murdoch St
off Lenzie St 60 D1
Muslin St 64 D4
Myreside Pl 65 H2
Myreside St 65 H2

N

Naburn Gate 64 A4
Nairn St 58 D5
Nansen St 59 G3
Napier Dr 58 B6
Napier Pl 58 B6
Napier Rd 58 B6
Napiershall La 59 F4
Napiershall Pl
off Napiershall St 59 F4
Napiershall St 59 F4
Napier Ter 58 B6
Nelson Mandela
Pl 60 A6
Nelson St 63 G2
Neptune St 62 B1
Nethan St 58 A6
Netherby Dr 62 D4
Netherfield St 65 G2
Newark Dr 62 D5
Newbank Gdns 65 H4
New City Rd 59 H5
Newhall St 64 C5
Newmill Rd 61 G1
Newton Pl 59 F5
Newton St
off Argyle St 59 G6
Newton Ter
off Sauchiehall St 59 F6
Newton Ter La 59 F6
New Wynd 64 A2
Nicholas St 64 B1
Nicholson La
off Nicholson St 63 H2
Nicholson St 63 H2
Niddrie Rd 63 F6
Niddrie Sq 63 F6
Nisbet St 65 H3
Nithsdale Dr 63 F6
Nithsdale Pl
off Nithsdale Rd 63 F5
Nithsdale Rd 63 F6
Nithsdale St 63 F6
Nith St 61 H5
Norfolk Ct 63 H3
Norfolk La
off Norfolk St 63 H3
Norfolk St 64 A3
Norman St 64 D5
North Canal Bk 60 A4
North Canal Bk St 60 A4
North Claremont
St
off Royal Ter 59 E5
North Ct
off St. Vincent Pl 64 A1
North Ct La
off Buchanan St 64 A1
Northcroft Rd 60 D2
North Dr 63 H1
North Frederick St 64 A1

North Gardner St 58 B4
North Gower St 62 C3
North Hanover Pl
off North Hanover
St 60 A6
North Hanover St 60 A6
Northpark St 59 F2
North Pl
off North St 59 F6
North Portland St 64 B1
North St 59 F6
Northumberland
St 59 E2
North Wallace St 60 B5
North Woodside
Rd 59 F3
Norval St 58 A4
Norwich Dr 58 B1
Novar Dr 58 A2
Nuneaton St 65 E5
Nuneaton St
Ind Est 65 E5
Nursery La 63 F6
Nursery St
off Pollokshaws
Rd 63 G5

O

Oakbank Ind Est 59 H3
Oakfield Av 59 E4
Oakfield La 59 E4
Oakley Ter 64 D1
Oak St 63 G1
Oatfield St 61 F2
Oban Ct
off Kelvinside
Gdns 59 E2
Oban Dr 59 E2
Oban La 59 E2
Observatory La
off Observatory
Rd 58 D3
Observatory Rd 58 C3
Ogilvie Pl 65 H4
Ogilvie St 65 H4
Old Dalmarnock
Rd 64 D4
Old Dumbarton
Rd 58 C5
Old Rutherglen
Rd 64 A4
Old Wynd 64 A2
Olive St 61 H2
Olympia St 64 D3
Onslow Dr 65 E1
Onslow Sq 65 E1
Oran Gdns 59 E1
Oran Gate 59 E1
Oran Pl 59 E2
Oran St 59 E1
Oregon Pl 64 A4
Orkney Pl
off Orkney St 62 A1
Orkney St 62 B1
Orr St 64 D3
Orton Pl 62 A2
Osborne St 64 A2
Oswald St 63 H2
Otago La 59 E4
Otago La N
off Otago St 59 E4
Otago St 59 E4
Overnewton Pl
off Kelvinhaugh St 58 D6
Overnewton Sq
off Blackie St 58 D5
Overnewton St 58 D5
Overtown Pl 65 E3
Overtown St 65 E3
Oxford La 63 H3
Oxford St 63 H2

P

Pacific Dr 62 C2
Pacific Quay 62 D1
Paisley Rd 63 G2

Paisley Rd W 62 C3
Palermo St
off Atlas Rd 60 C2
Palmerston Pl
off Kelvinhaugh St 58 D6
Panmure Cl 59 G2
Panmure St 59 G2
Park Av 59 F4
Park Circ 59 E5
Park Circ La 59 E5
Park Circ Pl 59 F5
Park Dr 59 E4
Park Gdns 59 E5
Park Gdns La 59 E5
Park Gate 59 E5
Parkgrove Ter 59 E5
Parkgrove Ter La
off Derby St 59 E5
Parkhead Cross 65 H3
Park Quad 59 E5
Park Rd 59 E4
Park St S 59 E5
Park Ter 59 E5
Park Ter E La 59 E5
Park Ter La 59 E5
Parnie St 64 A2
Parsonage Row 64 B1
Parsonage Sq 64 B1
Parson St 60 C6
Partick Br St 58 C4
Partickhill Av 58 B4
Partickhill Ct 58 B3
Partickhill Rd 58 B3
Paterson St 63 G3
Patna St 65 F5
Paton St 65 F1
Payne St 60 A4
Pearce La
off Pearce St 58 A6
Pearce St 58 A6
Peathill St 60 A3
Peel La 58 B4
Peel St 58 B4
Pembroke St 59 F6
Penicuik St 65 H2
Percy St
off Clifford St 62 D2
Perth St
off Argyle St 63 F1
Petershill Ct 61 G2
Petershill Dr 61 F2
Petershill Pl 61 F2
Petershill Rd 60 D3
Phoenix Pk Ter
off Corn St 59 H4
Phoenix Rd
off Great Western
Rd 59 G5
Piccadilly St 63 F1
Pine Pl 64 A4
Pinkston Dr 60 C4
Pinkston Rd 60 B3
Pitt St 63 G1
Plantation Pk Gdns
off Clifford La 62 D3
Plantation Sq 63 E2
Plant St 65 G2
Playfair St 65 E5
Pointhouse Rd 63 E1
Pollokshaws Rd 63 G6
Pollokshields Sq
off Glencairn Dr 63 F6
Polmadie Av 64 B6
Polmadie Ind Est 64 C6
Polmadie Rd 64 C5
Polwarth La 58 B2
Polwarth St 58 B3
Poplar Rd
off Urrdale Rd 62 B3
Poplin St 64 D5
Port Dundas
Ind Est 60 A4
Port Dundas Pl 60 A6
Port Dundas Rd 59 H5
Port Dundas
Trd Centres 60 A4

Porter St 62 C
Portman Pl
off Cowan St 59 E
Portman St 63 E
Port St 59 F
Portugal La
off Bedford St 63 H
Portugal St 63 H
Possil Cross 60 A
Possil Rd 59 H
Powfoot St 65 H
Preston Pl 63 H
Preston St 63 H
Prince Albert Rd 58 B
Prince Edward St 63 G
Prince's Dock 62 C
Princes Gdns 58 B
Princes Pl 58 C
Princes Sq
off Buchanan St 64 A
Princes Ter 58 C
Professors Sq 58 D
Provanhill St 60 D
Provanmill Pl
off Provanmill Rd 61 H
Provanmill Rd 61 H
Provan Rd 61 G
Purdon St 58 B

Q

Quarrybrae St 65 H
Quarrywood Av 61 G
Quarrywood Rd 61 H
Queen Elizabeth
Gdns 64 A
Queen Elizabeth
Sq 64 B
Queen Margaret Ct
off Fergus Dr 59 E
Queen Margaret
Dr 58 D
Queen Margaret
Rd 59 E
Queen Mary St 64 D
Queensborough
Gdns 58 A
Queens Cres 59 F
Queens Dr 63 F
Queensferry St 64 C
Queens Gdns
off Victoria Cres
Rd 58 C
Queens Gate La
off Victoria Cres
Rd 58 C
Queenslie St 61 H
Queens Pl 58 C
Queen Sq 63 F
Queen St 64 A

R

Radnor St
off Argyle St 58 D
Raeberry St 59 F
Rafford St 62 A
Raglan St 59 G
Rathlin St 58 A
Ratho Dr 60 C
Ravel Row 65 H
Ravelston St 65 H
Redan St 64 D
Redford St 61 H
Redlands La 58 C
Redlands Rd 58 C
Redlands Ter
off Julian Av 58 C
Redlands Ter La 58 C
Redmoss St 59 H
Rednock St 60 A
Red Rd 61 F
Red Rd Ct 61 F
Redwood Dr 61 E
Regent Moray St 58 D
Regent Pk Sq 63 F
Reidhouse St 60 D
Reid Pl 64 D

id St	64 D5
idvale St	64 D2
nfield La	
off Hope St	63 H1
nfield St	63 H1
nfrew St	59 H6
nfrew La	
off Hope St	59 H6
nfrew St	59 H6
nton St	60 A5
ymer St	60 C5
ynie Dr	62 B3
ccarton St	64 A6
chard St	
off Cadzow St	63 G1
chmond St	64 B1
msdale St	65 E3
ngford St	60 D3
tchie St	63 G4
verview Dr	63 G2
verview Gdns	63 G2
verview Pl	63 G2
obert Dr	58 A6
oberton Av	62 C6
obertson La	63 G1
obertson St	63 H1
obert St	58 A6
obson Gro	63 H5
ockbank Pl	65 E3
ockbank St	65 E3
ockcliffe St	64 D5
ockfield Pl	61 G1
ockfield Rd	61 G1
ock St	59 H3
odney St	59 H4
oebank St	61 F6
ogart St	64 D3
ona St	61 F4
opework La	
off Clyde St	64 A2
oseberry St	64 C5
osemount Cres	60 D6
osemount St	60 D5
ose St	59 H6
osevale St	58 A4
oslea Dr	65 E1
osneath St	58 A6
osslyn Ter	58 C2
oss St	64 B2
osyth Rd	64 C6
osyth St	64 C6
ottenrow	60 B6
ottenrow E	64 B1
owallan Gdns	58 A3
owallan La E	58 A3
owan Gdns	62 B4
owan Rd	62 B4
owchester St	65 E3
oxburgh La	
off Saltoun St	58 D3
oxburgh St	58 D3
oyal Bk Pl	
off Buchanan St	64 A1
oyal Cres	59 E6
oyal Ex Bldgs	
off Royal Ex Sq	64 A1
oyal Ex Ct	
off Queen St	64 A1
oyal Ex Sq	64 A1
oyal Ter	59 E5
oyal Ter La	59 E5
oystonhill	60 D5
oystonhill Pl	60 D5
oyston Rd	60 C5
oyston Sq	60 C5
oy St	60 B3
uby St	65 E4
uchill Pl	
off Ruchill St	59 F1
uchill St	59 E1
umford St	64 D5
upert St	59 F4
ushyhill St	61 E2
uskin La	59 E3
uskin Pl	59 E3
uskin Ter	59 E3

Russell St	64 D5
off Vine St	58 B4
Rutherglen Br	64 D5
Rutherglen Rd	64 B5
Ruthven La	58 D3
Ruthven St	58 D3
Rutland Ct	
off Govan Rd	63 E2
Rutland Cres	63 E2
Rutland Pl	63 E2
Ryebank Rd	61 G1
Rye Cres	61 F1
Ryefield Rd	61 F1
Ryehill Pl	61 G1
Ryehill Rd	61 G1
Ryemount Rd	61 F1
Rye Rd	61 F1
Ryeside Rd	61 F1

S

St. Andrews Cres	63 E4
St. Andrews Cross	63 G5
St. Andrews Dr	63 E4
St. Andrews La	
off Gallowgate	64 B2
St. Andrews Rd	63 F4
St. Andrews Sq	64 B2
St. Andrews St	64 B2
St. Clair St	
off North Woodside Rd	59 F4
St. Enoch Shop Cen	64 A2
St. Enoch Sq	63 H2
St. Francis Rigg	64 A4
St. Georges Ct	
off St. Georges Rd	59 G5
St. Georges Rd	59 G4
St. James Rd	60 B6
St. John's Ct	63 E4
St. John's Quad	63 E4
St. John's Rd	63 E5
St. Joseph's Ct	60 D5
St. Joseph's Pl	60 D5
St. Joseph's Vw	60 D5
St. Luke's Pl	64 A3
St. Luke's Ter	64 A3
St. Margarets Pl	
off Bridgegate	64 A2
St. Marnock St	65 E3
St. Marys La	
off West Nile St	63 H1
St. Michael's Ct	
off St. Michael's La	65 G3
St. Michael's La	65 G3
St. Monance St	60 D1
St. Mungo Av	60 A6
St. Mungo Pl	60 B6
St. Ninian Ter	
off Ballater St	64 A3
St. Peters La	
off Blythswood St	63 G1
St. Peter's Path	
off Braid St	59 G4
St. Peters St	59 G4
St. Rollox Brae	60 C4
St. Valentine Ter	64 B4
St. Vincent Cres	58 D6
St. Vincent Cres La	58 D6
St. Vincent La	
off Hope St	59 G6
St. Vincent Pl	64 A1
St. Vincent St	59 G6
St. Vincent Ter	59 F6
Salamanca St	65 H3
Salisbury Pl	63 H4
Salisbury St	63 H4
Salkeld St	63 H4
Salmona St	59 H2
Saltmarket	64 A2
Saltmarket Pl	
off Bridgegate	64 A2
Saltoun Gdns	
off Roxburgh St	58 D3

Saltoun La	58 D3
Saltoun St	58 C3
Sanda St	59 E2
Sandfield St	59 E1
Sandiefield Rd	64 A4
Sandmill St	61 E5
Sandringham La	
off Kersland St	58 D3
Sandyford Pl	59 F6
Sandyford Pl La	59 E6
Sandyford St	58 C6
Sandy La	
off Crawford St	58 A4
Sandy Rd	58 A5
Sannox Gdns	61 F6
Saracen Head La	
off Gallowgate	64 C2
Saracen St	60 A3
Sardinia La	58 D3
Sardinia Ter	
off Cecil St	58 D3
Sauchiehall La	
off Sauchiehall St	59 G6
Sauchiehall St	59 G6
Savoy St	64 D4
Sawmillfield St	59 H4
Schipka Pas	
off Gallowgate	64 B2
Scone St	60 A3
Scotland St	63 F3
Scotland St W	63 E3
Scotsburn Rd	61 G2
Scotstoun Mill Rd	
off Partick Br St	58 C5
Scott St	59 G6
Seagrove St	65 H2
Seamore St	59 F4
Seath St	64 A6
Seaward La	63 E2
Seaward Pl	63 E4
Seaward St	63 F3
Second Gdns	62 A4
Seton Ter	64 D1
Shaftesbury St	59 F6
Shakespeare St	59 E1
Shamrock St	59 G5
Shanks St	59 F1
Shannon St	59 F1
Shawfield Dr	64 C6
Shawfield Ind Est	64 D6
Shawfield Rd	64 D5
Shaw St	58 A6
Shearer St	
off Paisley Rd	63 F2
Shelley Ct	58 A1
Sheppard St	
off Cowlairs Rd	60 C2
Sherbrooke Av	62 C5
Sherbrooke Dr	62 C4
Sherbrooke Gdns	62 C5
Shettleston Rd	65 G2
Shields Rd	63 F3
Shipbank La	
off Clyde St	64 A2
Shore St	64 D6
Shortridge St	59 E1
Shuna Gdns	59 F1
Shuna Pl	59 E1
Shuttle La	
off George St	64 B1
Shuttle St	64 B1
Sidland Rd	61 G1
Siemens Pl	61 F4
Siemens St	61 F4
Silverdale St	65 G4
Silverfir Ct	64 B5
Silverfir Pl	64 B5
Silverfir St	64 B5
Silvergrove St	64 C3
Simpson St	59 F3
Skene Rd	62 B3
Slatefield Ct	
off Slatefield St	65 E2
Slatefield St	65 E2
Sloy St	60 B2

Snowdon Pl	
off Benthall St	64 B4
Snowdon St	
off Benthall St	64 B4
Society St	65 F3
Solway St	64 D6
Somerset Pl	59 F5
Somerset Pl Ms	59 F5
Sorby St	65 H3
Sorn St	65 F5
South Annandale St	63 H6
Southbank St	65 H3
Southcroft St	62 B1
South Ex Ct	
off Queen St	64 A1
South Frederick St	64 A1
Southloch Gdns	60 D3
Southloch St	60 D3
Southmuir Pl	58 D1
Southpark Av	58 D4
Southpark La	59 E4
Southpark Ter	
off Southpark Av	59 E4
South Portland St	63 H3
Southside Cres	63 H4
South Woodside Rd	59 F3
Spiers Wf	59 H4
Spoutmouth	
off Gallowgate	64 B2
Springbank St	59 F2
Springburn Rd	60 C4
Springburn Shop Cen	60 D2
Springburn Way	60 C2
Springfield Ct	
off Buchanan St	64 A1
Springfield Quay	63 F2
Springfield Rd	65 F5
Springkell Av	62 C5
Springkell Dr	62 B6
Springkell Gdns	62 C6
Springkell Gate	62 D6
Spring La	
off Lawmoor St	64 A5
Springvale Ter	60 C2
Spring Wynd	64 A4
Spruce St	60 B1
Staffa St	61 F6
Stafford St	60 B5
Stag St	62 B1
Stair St	59 F2
Stamford Pl	65 F3
Stamford Rd	65 F3
Stamford St	65 F3
Stanley St	63 E3
Stanley St La	63 E3
Steel St	64 B2
Stevenson St	64 C2
Stewart St	59 H5
Stewartville St	58 B4
Stirlingfauld Pl	63 H3
Stirling Rd	60 B6
Stobcross Rd	58 D6
Stobcross St	63 F1
Stobcross Wynd	58 C6
Stockwell Pl	64 A2
Stockwell St	64 A2
Stonyhurst St	59 H2
Stratford St	58 D1
Strathbran St	65 H4
Strathclyde St	65 E6
Striven Gdns	59 F3
Stroma St	61 F4
Stromness St	63 G4
Stronend St	59 H1
Stronsay St	61 F4
Suffolk St	
off Kent St	64 C2
Summerfield St	65 F6
Summer St	64 D3
Summertown Rd	62 B1
Sunnybank St	65 F5
Sunnylaw St	59 H2

Surrey St	63 H4
Sussex St	63 E3
Sutherland Av	62 B5
Sutherland La	58 C4
Swanston St	65 E6
Swan St	60 A5
Sword St	64 D2
Sydenham La	
off Crown Rd S	58 B3
Sydenham Rd	58 C3
Sydney St	64 C2
Syriam Pl	
off Syriam St	60 D2
Syriam St	60 D2

T

Tamworth St	
off Rimsdale St	65 E3
Tannock St	59 H2
Taransay St	58 A6
Taylor Pl	60 B6
Taylor St	64 B1
Telephone La	58 C3
Templetons Business Cen	64 C3
Templeton St	64 C3
Terregles Av	62 B6
Terregles Cres	62 B6
Terregles Dr	62 C6
Teviot St	58 C6
Teviot Ter	
off Sanda St	59 E2
Tharsis St	60 D5
Third Gdns	62 A4
Thistle St	64 A3
Thistle Ter	64 A4
Thomson St	65 E2
Thornbank St	58 C5
Thornbridge Av	
off Balcarres Av	58 C1
Thorncliffe Gdns	63 E6
Thorncliffe La	63 E6
Thornhill Path	
off Crail St	65 H4
Thornwood Av	58 A4
Thornwood Gdns	58 A4
Thornwood Pl	58 A3
Thurso St	58 C5
Tibbermore Rd	58 A3
Tillie St	59 F3
Tiree St	61 G4
Tobago Pl	64 C3
Tobago St	64 C3
Todd St	65 G1
Toll Ct	63 E2
Tollcross Rd	65 H3
Tontine La	64 B2
Torness St	58 C4
Torrance St	60 D2
Torr Gdns	60 B2
Torridon Av	62 B5
Torridon Path	
off Dumbreck Av	62 A5
Torrisdale St	63 F6
Torr Pl	60 B2
Torr St	60 B2
Torryburn Rd	61 G2
Toryglen St	64 B6
Tower St	63 E3
Townmill Rd	60 D6
Townsend St	60 A5
Tradeston St	63 G3
Trafalgar St	64 D5
Trongate	64 A2
Troon St	65 F5
Trossachs Ct	
off Trossachs St	59 G3
Trossachs St	59 G3
Tullis Ct	64 C4
Tullis St	64 C4
Tunnel St	63 E1
Tureen St	64 D2
Turnberry Av	
off Turnberry Rd	58 B3
Turnberry Rd	58 A3
Turnbull St	64 B2

Turner Rd 60 D4
Turnlaw St 64 B4
Turriff St 63 H4
Tweed Cres 61 H5
Tyndrum St 60 A5

U
Union Pl
  off Gordon St 63 H1
Union St 63 H1
Unity Pl 59 G4
University Av 58 D4
University Gdns 58 D4
University of
  Glasgow 58 D4
University Pl 58 D4
Urrdale Rd 62 B3

V
Valleyfield St
  off Ayr St 60 C3
Vasart Pl 59 F1
Vennard Gdns 63 E6
Vermont St 63 E3
Vicarfield Pl
  off Vicarfield St 62 B1
Vicarfield St 62 B1
Victoria Br 64 A2
Victoria Circ 58 C3
Victoria Cres
  off Dowanside Rd 58 C3
Victoria Cres La 58 C3
Victoria Cres Pl
  off Bowmont Ter 58 C3
Victoria Cres Rd 58 C3
Victoria Cross 63 G6
Viewfield La 59 E4
Viewpark Av 61 F6
Vine St 58 B4
Vinicombe La 58 D3
Vinicombe St 58 D3
Vintner St 60 A4
Virginia Bldgs
  off Virginia St 64 A1

Virginia Ct
  off Virginia St 64 A1
Virginia Pl 64 A1
Virginia St 64 A1
Vulcan St
  off Springburn
  Way 60 C2

W
Waddell Ct 64 B3
Waddell St 64 B4
Walker Ct 58 B5
Walker St 58 B5
Walkinshaw St 65 E4
Wallace St 63 G2
Wallacewell Cres 61 F1
Wallacewell Pl 61 F1
Wallacewell Rd 61 F1
Walls St 64 B1
Walmer Cres 62 C2
Walnut Cres 60 B1
Walnut Pl 60 B1
Walnut Rd 60 B1
Walter St 65 F1
Wanlock St 58 A6
Wardhill Rd 61 F1
Wardrop St 58 A6
Warnock St 60 C6
Warriston Cres 61 H6
Warriston St 61 H6
Warroch St 63 F1
Washington St 63 G1
Waterloo La
  off Waterloo St 63 H1
Waterloo St 63 G1
Water Row 58 A6
Waterside Pl 64 B4
Waterside St 64 B4
Watson St 64 B2
Watt St 63 F2
Waverley Ter
  off Whitevale St 65 E2
Weaver St 64 B1
Webster St 65 E5

Wellcroft Pl 63 H4
Wellfield St 60 D2
Wellington La 63 G1
Wellington St 63 H1
Wellpark St 64 C1
Westbank Ct 59 E4
Westbank La 59 E4
Westbank Quad 59 E4
Westbourne
  Gdns La 58 C2
Westbourne
  Gdns N 58 C2
Westbourne
  Gdns S 58 C2
Westbourne
  Gdns W 58 C2
Westbourne Rd 58 B2
Westbourne Ter La
  Rd 58 B2
West Campbell St 63 G1
West End Pk St 59 F5
Wester Common
  Dr 59 G1
Wester Common
  Rd 59 G2
Wester Common
  Ter 59 H2
Westercraigs 64 D1
Westercraigs Ct
  off Westercraigs 64 D1
West George La
  off Pitt St 59 G6
West George St 59 G6
West Graham St 59 G5
West Greenhill Pl 59 E6
Westminster Gdns
  off Kersland St 58 D3
Westminster Ter
  off Royal Ter 59 E6
Westmoreland St 63 G6
Westmuir St 65 H3
West Nile St 63 H1
West Princes St 59 F4

West Regent La
  off Hope St 59 H6
West Regent St 59 G6
Westside Gdns 58 B4
West St 63 G3
West Whitby St 65 G4
Whitefield Rd 62 C3
Whitehall St 63 F1
Whitehill Ct 65 E1
Whitehill Gdns 65 E1
Whitehill Pl 65 E1
Whitehill St 65 E1
Whitehill St La 65 E1
White St 58 B4
Whitevale St 65 E2
Whittingehame
  Gdns 58 A1
Whitworth Gate 59 G1
Williamson St 65 G4
William St 59 F6
Willowbank Cres
  off Woodlands Rd 59 F4
Willowbank St 59 F4
Wilson St 64 A1
Wilton Cres 59 F3
Wilton Cres La 59 F3
Wilton Dr 59 F3
Wilton Gdns 59 F3
Wilton St 59 E3
Windmillcroft
  Quay 63 G2
Windsor St 59 G4
Windsor Ter 59 G4
Winifred St 61 H2
Winning Row 65 H3
Winton Dr 58 C1
Winton La 58 C1
Wishart St 64 C1
Woddrop St 65 F6
Wolseley St 64 B5
Woodhall St 65 F6
Woodlands Dr 59 F4
Woodlands Gate 59 F5
Woodlands Rd 59 F4

Woodlands Ter 59 E5
Woodrow Circ 62 D4
Woodrow Pl 62 C4
Woodrow Rd 62 D4
Woodside Cres 59 F5
Woodside Pl 59 F5
Woodside Pl La 59 F5
Woodside Ter 59 F5
Woodside Ter La 59 F5
Wood St 61 F6
Woodville Pk 62 B2
Woodville St 62 B2
Wyndford Dr 58 D1
Wyndford Pl
  off Wyndford Rd 58 D1
Wyndford Rd 58 C1
Wyndham Ct
  off Wyndham St 58 D2
Wyndham St 58 D2
Wyper Pl 65 E2

Y
Yarrow Gdns 59 F3
Yarrow Gdns La
  off Yarrow Gdns 59 F3
Yate Gro 65 F3
Yate Rd 65 F3
Yate St 65 F3
Yew Dr 61 E3
Yorkhill Par 58 C5
Yorkhill Quay 58 B6
Yorkhill St 58 D6
York St 63 G2
Young Ter 61 E2

Z
Zena Cres 61 G2
Zena Pl 61 H2
Zena St 61 H2